AngularJS Directives

Learn how to craft dynamic directives to fuel your
single-page web applications using AngularJS

Alex Vanston

[PACKT] open source
PUBLISHING   community experience distilled

BIRMINGHAM - MUMBAI

AngularJS Directives

Copyright © 2013 Packt Publishing

First published: August 2013

Production Reference: 1200813

Published by Packt Publishing Ltd.
Livery Place
35 Livery Street
Birmingham B3 2PB, UK.

ISBN 978-1-78328-033-9

www.packtpub.com

Cover Image by Eleanor Leonne Bennett (eleanor.ellieonline@gmail.com)

Credits

Author
Alex Vanston

Reviewers
Jeff Cunningham

Brian Petro

Acquisition Editor
Rukhsana Khambatta

Commissioning Editor
Subho Gupta

Technical Editors
Manan Badani

Monica John

Sampreshita Maheshwari

Project Coordinator
Michelle Quadros

Proofreader
Stephen Silk

Indexer
Tejal R. Soni

Graphics
Abhinash Sahu

Production Coordinator
Conidon Miranda

Cover Work
Conidon Miranda

About the Author

Alex Vanston is a self-professed geek and an outdoor junkie fused together. During high-school he began teaching himself how to code and has been obsessed with learning new languages and better ways to solve problems ever since. He has been building web sites and applications professionally for the past seven years, for clients and companies around the world. Currently he lives in Denver, CO, where he loves hiking (5 14ers down, 49 to go), playing pickup sports, and water skiing when he can. He's the lead front-end developer for ZipKick, Inc, a travel startup taking off in San Francisco, CA. You can find him online at http://www.mrvdot.com, where he blogs about web development and tech.

A huge thank you to the innumerable friends and family who have encouraged me through this writing process, listened to me wrestle with word choice and politely ignored me when I inexplicably begin monologuing at random moments when a new idea hit me.

About the Reviewers

Jeff Cunningham is a mobile developer for The General Insurance. After 15 years of Java web development, he is now enjoying the challenges of front-end and mobile web development. Prior to working for The General, Jeff worked at The Weather Channel where he was able to use both of his college degrees: Atmospheric Science and Computer Science. When not programming, Jeff enjoys reading, spending time with his family, and watching sports.

Brian Petro has long been a proponent of AngularJS. He has curated a handful of developer resources dedicated to Angular. For example, 'Angular Developers' is a group on LinkedIn where users can access the latest community generated material. Through these experiences, Brian observed a significant deficit of talent in this fast growing field. AngularJobs.com is a place where developers find opportunities to work with Angular.

> I would like to thank the author for providing a much needed resource on this topic.

www.PacktPub.com

Support files, eBooks, discount offers and more

You might want to visit www.PacktPub.com for support files and downloads related to your book.

Did you know that Packt offers eBook versions of every book published, with PDF and ePub files available? You can upgrade to the eBook version at www.PacktPub.com and as a print book customer, you are entitled to a discount on the eBook copy. Get in touch with us at service@packtpub.com for more details.

At www.PacktPub.com, you can also read a collection of free technical articles, sign up for a range of free newsletters and receive exclusive discounts and offers on Packt books and eBooks.

http://PacktLib.PacktPub.com

Do you need instant solutions to your IT questions? PacktLib is Packt's online digital book library. Here, you can access, read and search across Packt's entire library of books.

Why Subscribe?

- Fully searchable across every book published by Packt
- Copy and paste, print and bookmark content
- On demand and accessible via web browser

Free Access for Packt account holders

If you have an account with Packt at www.PacktPub.com, you can use this to access PacktLib today and view nine entirely free books. Simply use your login credentials for immediate access.

Table of Contents

Preface

AngularJS Directives dives into the core building blocks of Angular.JS and provides you with the knowledge you need to create fully dynamic web applications that respond in real time to updates and changes in your data. You'll learn how to build directives from the ground up, as well as some of the best practices to use when architecting them. By the end you'll be able to create a web application comprised of multiple modules all working together seamlessly to provide the best possible user experience.

What this book covers

Chapter 1, Designing Web Applications in 2013, provides a quick introduction to single-page web applications and the current best practices for developing them.

Chapter 2, The Need for Directives, discusses the value of Angular.JS directives and how they satisfy many of the best practices discussed in *Chapter 1, Designing Web Applications in 2013*.

Chapter 3, Deconstructing Directives, highlights each of the configuration options available for directives and provides examples of how they can be used.

Chapter 4, Compile versus Link, dives into the two separate processes by which Angular.JS parses and transforms static HTML into a series of directives and dynamic elements.

Chapter 5, Keeping it Clean with Scope, serves as a study into the different degrees of scoping and isolation that AngularJS provides for its directives.

Chapter 6, Controllers – Better with Sharing, discusses the advantages of using controllers to coordinate between parent and child directives.

Chapter 7, Transclusion, provides an overview for consuming existing HTML content into your directive while preserving the appropriate scopes.

Chapter 8, Good Karma – Testing in Angular, introduces the Karma test-runner and provides an overview of best practices for testing Angular applications.

Chapter 9, A Deeper Dive into Unit Testing, dives deeper into the realm of unit testing and discusses the Angular approach to validating functionality.

Chapter 10, Bringing it All Together, walks through the creation of a custom Angular.JS directive from beginning to end.

What you need for this book

To follow along with the examples, you'll need a standard text editor or IDE of your choice. A basic web server such as Apache isn't required, but highly recommended, particularly for the chapter on E2E testing. Some basic command-line knowledge is recommended, but all the steps required will be explicitly written out within the text.

Who this book is for

This book is intended for intermediate JavaScript developers who are looking to enhance their understanding of single-page web application development, with a focus on Angular.JS and the JavaScript MVC framework. It is expected that you will understand basic JavaScript patterns and idioms and can recognize JSON formatted data, however, no prior MVC or Angular.JS knowledge is required.

Conventions

In this book, you will find a number of styles of text that distinguish between different kinds of information. Here are some examples of these styles, and an explanation of their meaning.

Code words in text are shown as follows: "With this approach, our JavaScript is nothing more than a function (attached to our element via `ng-controller="WidgetController"`) that binds our tweets to a `$scope` object "

A block of code is set as follows:

```
$('#nextLink').click(function () {
  $.get('api/next', function (nextPage) {
    displayPage(nextPage);
  })
});
```

When we wish to draw your attention to a particular part of a code block, the relevant lines or items are set in bold:

```
<p ng-repeat="tweet in tweets" tweet>
  <!-- ng-click allows us to bind a click event to a function on the
  $scope object -->
  @{{tweet.author}}: {{tweet.text}} <span ng-
  click="retweet()">RT</span> | <span ng-
  click="reply()">Reply</span>
</p>
```

New terms and **important words** are shown in bold. Words that you see on the screen, in menus or dialog boxes for example, appear in the text like this: "clicking the **Next** button moves you to the next screen".

 Warnings or important notes appear in a box like this.

Tips and tricks appear like this.

Reader feedback

Feedback from our readers is always welcome. Let us know what you think about this book—what you liked or may have disliked. Reader feedback is important for us to develop titles that you really get the most out of.

To send us general feedback, simply send an e-mail to feedback@packtpub.com, and mention the book title via the subject of your message.

If there is a topic that you have expertise in and you are interested in either writing or contributing to a book, see our author guide on www.packtpub.com/authors.

Customer support

Now that you are the proud owner of a Packt book, we have a number of things to help you to get the most from your purchase.

Downloading the example code

You can download the example code files for all Packt books you have purchased from your account at http://www.packtpub.com. If you purchased this book elsewhere, you can visit http://www.packtpub.com/support and register to have the files e-mailed directly to you.

Errata

Although we have taken every care to ensure the accuracy of our content, mistakes do happen. If you find a mistake in one of our books—maybe a mistake in the text or the code—we would be grateful if you would report this to us. By doing so, you can save other readers from frustration and help us improve subsequent versions of this book. If you find any errata, please report them by visiting http://www.packtpub.com/submit-errata, selecting your book, clicking on the **errata submission form** link, and entering the details of your errata. Once your errata are verified, your submission will be accepted and the errata will be uploaded on our website, or added to any list of existing errata, under the Errata section of that title. Any existing errata can be viewed by selecting your title from http://www.packtpub.com/support.

Piracy

Piracy of copyright material on the Internet is an ongoing problem across all media. At Packt, we take the protection of our copyright and licenses very seriously. If you come across any illegal copies of our works, in any form, on the Internet, please provide us with the location address or website name immediately so that we can pursue a remedy.

Please contact us at copyright@packtpub.com with a link to the suspected pirated material.

We appreciate your help in protecting our authors, and our ability to bring you valuable content.

Questions

You can contact us at questions@packtpub.com if you are having a problem with any aspect of the book, and we will do our best to address it.

1
Designing Web Applications in 2013

The goal of this chapter is to provide a quick introduction to some principles that will help you create high quality code, specifically aimed at frontend web application development. For a fuller study, I strongly recommend the article, *Patterns For Large-Scale JavaScript Application Architecture*, by *Addy Osmani*.

An overview of good code

If you're reading this book, I'm going to assume you've done at least some programming work yourself, likely more than a little. During that time, I hope you've had the chance to see some great code. Perhaps it was your own, but more likely, at least for the first couple times you glimpsed it, it was someone else's masterpiece. You probably didn't necessarily know what made it great; you just knew that it was far better than anything you had ever been able to extract out of a keyboard.

On the other hand, almost anyone can identify bad code (unless it's their own, but that's a whole different book). The logical holes, the ignored errors, the horrifyingly inconsistent indentation; we've seen it all, often with our own name attached to the file, but somehow transforming that spaghetti mess into anything resembling those works of art that we'd previously marveled at continues to escape us. This book isn't about beautiful code, but it is about a framework which flexes its muscles most effectively when wielded in a manner optimized for frontend applications, and as such it's worthwhile for us to spend a chapter discussing some of the best practices for modern frontend web development.

For the purposes of our overview, we'll look at two basic tenets: **modularity** and **data driven development**. Before we examine those, however, I want to use the next section to address a common misunderstanding about frontend web development: adding more APIs is not always the answer.

We're not just talking about a lot of APIs

Often, when a backend developer first begins working on a frontend project, they believe that they can simply create an awesome API in the backend, call it with the frontend code, and have a complete frontend web application. When I first started developing frontend web applications, I wrote a lot of code that looked like the following:

```
$('#nextLink').click(function () {
  $.get('api/next', function (nextPage) {
    displayPage(nextPage);
  })
});
```

While the frontend technically handles both the user interaction (`$('#nextLink').click()`), and the display (`displayPage(nextPage)`), the real driver here is the backend API. The API handles the logic, the state, and makes nearly all the decisions about how the application should actually function.

In contrast, the frontend applications built on top of data modeling frameworks allow us to move away from that paradigm and instead position the client-side code as the primary driver. This is awesome for two reasons:

1. It allows modern web developers to do 90 percent of the coding in the same language. This creates the potential for more code reuse, easier debugging, and all-round more efficient development, since even developers who speak both client and server-side languages fluently will lose some momentum when they have to switch between them.

2. The user experience vastly improves when everything we need to run the application is already downloaded and available. Because the majority of the logic and application processing is done client side, we are no longer dependent upon network requests or additional downloads before moving the user forward. And as the JavaScript engines in all modern browsers get continually faster with each release, even computationally intense processes are becoming less and less of a limiting factor.

These reasons can make a significant difference in even the smallest of applications, even if it's only in your own peace of mind while developing. As you begin to tackle larger projects, however, especially if you're working on a distributed team, modular code that all builds on top of the same data-model becomes mission-critical; without it, each bit of functionality might expect a different property, flag, or (brace yourself) classname to represent the appropriate state for your application. In contrast, when your code is data-driven, everyone can work off the same built-in value map, allowing different pieces to connect far more seamlessly.

Now that we've clarified what frontend development isn't, let's gets back to the key principles that lead to great frontend application code.

Modularity

The principle of modularity is hardly specific to frontend web applications, and most developers these days recognize its usefulness, so I won't spend a lot of time here, but it's worth a quick overview.

The primary goal of modularity is to ensure that the code you write can be reused in different parts of the same application, or even in different applications entirely, without requiring extensive re-architecting. This also helps ensure that a change to the internal logic of one feature doesn't negatively impact the functionality of any other. In his article, *Patterns For Large-Scale JavaScript Application Architecture*, *Addy Osmani* describes it as:

> *Decouple app. architecture w/module, facade & mediator patterns. Mods publish msgs, mediator acts as pub/sub mgr & facade handles security.*

In non-twitter speak, the basic goal is to make sure each feature/module keeps track of its own data/state/existence, is not dependent on the behavior of any other module to perform its own functionality, and uses messages to alert other modules to its own changes and appropriately respond to the changes of others.

We'll dive into modularity in great detail in the coming chapters, as it's one of the core principles of Angular Directives, so for now we'll leave this summary here, and continue to the next key principle for frontend web applications.

Data driven development

There are several different X-driven development ideologies in the world of software and web development, test-driven and behavior-driven being two of the most popular. **data driven development** (**DDD** from here on out) doesn't preclude any of these, and actually works simultaneously with many of them quite easily. DDD simply means using the structure of the data (or the model) as the foundation from which you build and make all other development design decisions. This is most easily explained by looking at an example, so let's start here, and then we will reverse the process to create a new application in the coming chapters.

In this example, we've created the quintessential frontend widget, a twitter feed display. This also serves as a good moment to highlight that not all web applications have to fill the entire page. Often, a web app is a simple widget like this, possibly something that can be embedded in third-party sites, and while there are some differences in structure, the basic organization and guidelines are still the same.

First, a quick snippet of some JSON data that we might use for this widget (we won't worry about the actual retrieving of data from Twitter right now):

```
[
  {
    "author" : "mrvdot",
    "text" : "Check out my new Angular widget!",
  },
  {
    "author" : "mrvdot",
    "text" : "I love directives!"
  }
  ...
]
```

The HTML:

```
<div ng-controller="WidgetController">
  <h3>My Tweets</h3>
  <p ng-repeat="tweet in tweets">
    @{{tweet.author}}: {{tweet.text}}
  </p>
</div>
```

And finally the JavaScript:

```
function WidgetController ($scope) {
  $scope.tweets = [];//loaded from JSON data above
}
```

While the preceding example does operate within the Angular framework, the basic structure here is representative of all good frontend architectures.

Let's first take a high-level view of what's happening here. The first thing to note is that the data itself is most important. I listed it first not because it was shortest, but to illustrate that the data is the foundation from which the rest of the code evolves. After the data, we move onto the HTML. This is most applicable in Angular, though it applies to other frameworks as well. In this model, once we have the data, we use the HTML to describe the view, how we want to display the data, and also (jQuery aficionados, brace yourselves) how we want the user to interact with that data. Only then, at the end, do we write the little JavaScript code needed to glue it all together as the controller. From here, let's walk through it stepwise to see how everything works together.

Loading the data

When we first initialize our application, the first thing we need to do is load our data. In Angular, this is most commonly done through a service, which, while a vital part of Angular development, is outside the scope of this book. For now, let's just assume that we've already loaded our data into `$scope.tweets`. We'll dissect `$scope` in great detail later in *Chapter 5, Keeping it Clean with Scope*, so for the purpose of this example, just know that it serves as the link between the view and our data.

Structuring our HTML

Let's revisit the main element of our widget, the tweet paragraph tag:

```
<p ng-repeat="tweet in tweets">
  @{{tweet.author}}: {{tweet.text}}
</p>
```

The first part of the HTML code uses the `ng-repeat` attribute to declare (again, remember we're building our HTML on top of the data-model, not receiving a model and remolding the HTML to reflect it) that we want to iterate through the array of tweets and print out for each the author's handle and their tweets in a paragraph tag.

Adding JavaScript

Finally, because we've focused on building the HTML on top of the data itself, our JavaScript is only a few lines:

```
function WidgetController ($scope) {
  $scope.tweets = [];//loaded from JSON data
}
```

With this approach, our JavaScript is nothing more than a function (attached to our element via `ng-controller="WidgetController"`) that binds our tweets to a `$scope` object. We'll discuss the specifics of scopes and controllers later, for now just know that the scope serves as a bridge between the controller and our HTML.

Consider how we might have done this with jQuery (or a similar DOM manipulation library). First we'd have to iterate through all of the tweets and build the HTML string to insert into the message list. Then we'd need to watch for any new changes to our tweet array, at minimum append or prepend new items, or possibly rebuild the entire list if we can't rely on all our tweets coming in order.

Don't misunderstand, jQuery is an amazing library, and we'll go into extensive detail about how to use it in conjunction with Angular in the chapter on linking. The problem, however, is that jQuery was never designed to be a data-model interaction layer. It's great for the DOM manipulation, but trying to keep track of the DOM and the data at the same time gets tricky very quickly, and as anyone who has previously built an application using this structure can attest, adequate testing is nearly impossible.

Summary

Hopefully by now you're beginning to see that frontend web applications are far more than just a collection of Ajax calls with a master backend still running the show. And as such, principles such as modularity and data driven development are vital to successful and efficient development. Modularity helps us plug features together without worrying about undocumented interactions breaking our entire app. And DDD ensures that every bit of our code stands on the foundation of the data-model itself, so we can be confident that the user's view and interactions accurately reflect the true state of the application.

If you're still not convinced about everything, that's ok, we'll explore both of these principles in more detail throughout the coming chapters. For now, though, let's take the next chapter to explore what distinguishes Angular.JS from many of the other common JavaScript MVC frameworks available today.

2
The Need for Directives

This chapter could almost as easily be titled "The Need for Angular", as directives make up the heart and soul of what distinguishes Angular from other JavaScript libraries and frameworks. Certainly there are other key features, Dependency Injection being one of my favorites that makes it exemplary, however none are quite as foundational to Angular as directives.

With that in mind, let's take a look at what attributes define directives and why they're best suited for frontend development, as well as what makes them different from the JavaScript techniques and packages you've likely used earlier. Hopefully, by the end you'll understand a few of the key qualities that make directives ideal for frontend web development.

What makes a directive a directive

Angular directives have several distinguishing features, but for the sake of simplicity we'll focus on just three in this chapter. In contrast to most plugins or other forms of drop-in functionality, directives are **declarative**, **data driven**, and **conversational**.

Directives are declarative

If you've done any JavaScript development before, you've almost certainly used jQuery (or perhaps Prototype), and likely one of the thousands of plugins available for it. Perhaps you've even written your own such plugin. In either case, you probably have a decent understanding of the flow required to integrate it. They all look something like the following code:

```
$(document).ready(function() {
  $('#myElement').myPlugin({pluginOpts});
});
```

In short, we're finding the DOM element matching `#myElement`, then applying our jQuery plugin to it. These frameworks are built from the ground up on the principle of DOM manipulation. In contrast, as you may have noticed in the previous chapter, Angular directives are declarative, meaning we write them into the HTML elements themselves. Declarative programming means that instead of telling an object how to behave (imperative programming), we describe what an object is. So, where in jQuery we might grab an element and apply certain properties or behaviors to it, with Angular we label that element as a type of directive, and, elsewhere, maintain code that defines what properties and behaviors make up that type of object:

```html
<html>
  <body>
    <div id="myElement" my-awesome-directive></div>
  </body>
</html>
```

At a first glance, this may seem rather pedantic, merely a difference in styles, but as we begin to make our applications more complex, this approach serves to streamline many of the usual development headaches.

Consider again our example of the tweet list from the previous chapter. In a more fully developed application, our messages would likely be interactive, and in addition to growing or shrinking during the course of the user's visit, we'd want them to be able to reply to some or retweet themselves. If we were to implement this with a DOM manipulation library (such as jQuery or Prototype), that would require rebuilding the HTML with each change (assuming you want it sorted, just using `.append()` won't be enough), and then rebinding to each of the appropriate elements to allow the various interactions.

In contrast, if we use Angular directives, this all becomes much simpler. As before, we use the `ng-repeat` directive to watch our list and handle the iterated display of tweets, so any changes to our scoped array will automatically be reflected within the DOM. Additionally, we can create a simple tweet directive to handle the messaging interactions, starting with the following basic definition. Don't worry right now about the specific syntax of creating a directive, we'll cover that more in the next chapter; for now just take a look at the overall flow in the following code:

```
angular.module('myApp', [])
  .directive('tweet', ['api', function (api) {
    return function ($scope, $element, $attributes) {
      $scope.retweet = function () {
        api.retweet($scope.tweet);// Each scope inherits from it's
  parent, so we still have access to the full tweet object of {
  author : '…', text : '…' }
      };
```

```
        $scope.reply = function () {
          api.replyTo($scope.tweet);
        };
      }
    }]);
```

For now just know that we're getting an instance of our Twitter API connection and passing it into the directive in the variable `api`, then using that to handle the replies and retweets. Our HTML for each message now looks like the following code:

```
<p ng-repeat="tweet in tweets" tweet>
  <!-- ng-click allows us to bind a click event to a function on the
  $scope object -->
  @{{tweet.author}}: {{tweet.text}}
  <span ng-click="retweet()">RT</span> |
  <span ng-click="reply()">Reply</span>
</p>
```

By adding the `tweet` attribute to the paragraph tag, we tell Angular that this element should use the tweet directive, which gives us access to the published methods, as well as anything else we later decide to attach to the `$scope` object.

> Directives in Angular can be declared in multiple ways, including classes and comments, though attributes are the most common. We'll discuss the pros and cons of each method in the next chapter.

Scoping within directives is simultaneously one of the most powerful and most complicated features within Angular, so we'll spend all of *Chapter 5, Keeping it Clean with Scope* on it, but for now it's enough to know that every property and function we attach to the scope is accessible to us within the HTML declarations.

Directives are data driven

We talked in the previous chapter about how important being data driven is for frontend applications. Angular directives are built from the ground up with this philosophy. The scope and attribute objects accessible to each directive form the skeleton around which the rest of a directive is built and can be monitored for changes both within the DOM as well as the rest of your JavaScript code.

What this means for developers is that we no longer have to constantly poll for changes, or ensure that every data change that might have an impact elsewhere within our application is properly broadcast. Instead, the scope object handles all data changes for us, and because directives are declarative as well, that data is already connected to the elements of the view that need to update when the data changes. There's a proposal for ECMAScript 6 to support this kind of data watching natively with `Object.observe()`, but until that is implemented and fully supported, Angular's scope provides the much needed intermediary.

Directives are conversational

As we discussed in the previous chapter, modular coding emphasizes the use of messages to communicate between separate building blocks within an application. You're likely familiar with DOM events, used by many plugins to broadcast internal changes (for example, `save`, `initialized`, and so on) and subscribe to external events (for example, `click`, `focus`, and so on). Angular directives have access to all those events as well (the `$element` variable you saw earlier is actually a jQuery wrapped DOM element), but `$scope` also provides an additional messaging system that functions only along the scope tree. The `$emit` and `$broadcast` methods serve to send messages up and down the scope tree respectively, and like DOM events, allow directives to subscribe to changes or events within other parts of the application, while still remaining modular and uncoupled from the specific logic used to implement those changes.

 If you don't have jQuery included in your application, Angular wraps the element in jqLite, which is a lightweight wrapper that provides the same basic methods.

Additionally, when you add in the use of Angular services, which aren't the focus of this book but we'll touch on briefly in the next chapter, directives gain an even greater vocabulary. Services, among many other things, allow you to share specific pieces of data between the different pieces of your application, such as a collection of user preferences or utility mapping item codes to their names. Between this shared data and the messaging methods, separate directives are able to communicate fully with each other without requiring a retooling of their internal architecture.

Directives are everything you've dreamed about

Ok, that might be a bit of hyperbole, but you've probably noticed by now that the benefits outlined so far here are exactly in line with the best practices we discussed in the previous chapter. One of the most common criticisms of Angular is that it's relatively new (especially compared to frameworks such as Backbone and Ember). In contrast, however, I consider that to be one of its greatest assets. Older frameworks all defined themselves largely before there was a consensus on how frontend web applications should be developed. Angular, on the other hand, has had the advantage of being defined after many of the existing best practices had been established, and in my opinion provides the cleanest interface between an application's data and its display.

As we've seen already, directives are essentially data driven modules. They allow developers to easily create a packageable feature that declaratively attaches to an element, molds to fit the data at its disposal, and communicates with the other directives around it to ensure coordinated functionality without disruption of existing features.

Summary

In this chapter we learned about what attributes define directives and why they're best suited for frontend development, as well as what makes them different from the JavaScript techniques and packages you've likely used before. I realize that's a bold statement, and likely one that you don't fully believe yet. That's ok, we still have nine more chapters to go. Next we'll spend some time discussing just how to go about creating a directive and what some of the options mean, and hopefully you'll begin to see just how flexible, yet powerful, these directives can be.

3

Deconstructing Directives

And without further ado: Directives! Now that we've had the chance to discuss some of the *whys* of directives, let's get on with the *hows*. In this chapter, we'll go over each of the different configuration options you have at your disposal while creating a directive, as well as when each property is most helpful. Hopefully by the end of this chapter you'll begin to have a better understanding of what actually happens when we add a directive to an element and be excited to dive into some of the more powerful, but complex, configurations possible that are coming in the following chapters.

Getting started

If you've worked with Angular before, feel free to skip the next section, it's simply a review of how to set up an Angular.JS application and import other modules. We'll get into the specifics of directives in the *With directives* section.

With Angular

An Angular.JS application is first brought to life using the `angular.module` command, which is actually much more powerful than what we'll cover here. For the purpose of our text, we'll simply look at how to create a module and how to include other modules as you need. For a fuller read, the documentation on `angularjs.org` is actually pretty robust at `http://docs.angularjs.org/guide/module`.

Angular uses modules to separate different pieces of your application for easier testing and modularity. The recommended approach is to have separate modules for your services, directives, and filters, and one application-level module that imports all of them and then executes your initialization code, if any.

With this in mind, here's a quick example of what it looks like, and then we'll walk through it.

First, the JavaScript needed to initialize our module:

```
angular.module('myApp', ['myApp.directives']);
angular.module('myApp.directives', []);
```

Then the HTML code that tells Angular we want our page to be dynamically controlled:

```
<html ng-app="myApp">
  <head></head>
  <body></body>
</html>
```

A couple points to notice.

1. First, we don't need to wrap the `angular.module` statements within any sort of the `$(document).ready()` event listener. As long as the module file is loaded after Angular itself, Angular takes care of making sure everything is ready before charging forward.

2. Secondly, in that same vein, note that we can actually require a module before it's loaded. The array passed in as the second parameter to `angular.module` tells Angular what other module(s) should be required before initializing our new module, and in our case here, the directives module actually comes after our main `myApp` module (and could be in an entirely different file, loaded several requests later), however Angular waits until all the modules have been loaded before initializing any of them.

3. Finally, we use yet another directive, `ng-app` to tell Angular that this module is our primary module, please initialize it and then parse all the nodes within it. The `ng-app` directive can be attached to any DOM node, however, unless you're creating a small widget to be embedded within a different application, most commonly you'll want to use it on the `html` node itself.

> At the time of writing, when developing for Internet Explorer 8 & 9 browsers, the ng-app directive must be declared twice if you attach it to the html node. In addition to using the attribute to declare which module to use, you must also add the id tag of "ngApp", otherwise IE won't notice it during the bootstrap process.

As a closing note, for convenience' sake, Angular allows you also to retrieve a module by calling `angular.module` with just the name parameter (that is `angular.module('myApp')`), which can be helpful if you want to attach additional directives or other configurations to a directive in a separate file, or perhaps conditionally based on your environment variables.

With directives

Now that you have a basic understanding of how to initialize an Angular module, let's extend our directives module to demonstrate how to declare a directive within our code as shown:

```
...
angular.module('myApp.directives', [])
  .directive('myAwesomeDirective', function (){});
```

Obviously, this directive won't do much (and will actually throw an error if you try to use it because it's not complete yet), but this, in a nutshell, is how you create a directive. The .directive method on each module is actually a shortcut method to the same method on compileProvider, which you can use within a module's configuration block, but that's outside the goals of this book.

As mentioned earlier, our directive, as it stands right now, will actually throw an error if you try to attach it to a node, which is because Angular recognizes the directive, but doesn't know what to do with it. The function that makes up the second parameter isn't actually the directive definition in itself, but rather a factory, used to create the directive. This is a pattern common within Angular, and you'll see it used in controllers, services, and filters when you go on to create those. What this means is that the first time Angular needs to initialize your directive, it executes this factory function, then stores the result for all the future instances of the directive. As such, it's what we return from this factory function that actually determines the directive's configuration. This can be a bit confusing to discuss, but hopefully will make more sense as we continue our example as shown:

```
...
angular.module('myApp.directives', [])
  .directive('myAwesomeDirective', ['api', function(api) {
    //Do any one-time directive initialization work here
    return function($scope, $element, $attrs) {
      //Do directive work that needs to be applied to each
  instance here
    };
  }]);
```

Within your factory function, you can either return another function, as we did here, or a configuration object, which we'll go over in detail later in this chapter. The function accepts the current scope for the instance of that directive, the jQuery wrapped DOM element, and any attributes attached to the element as parameters, and often that will be all you'll need to use for your directive. This function gets called each time the directive is attached to a DOM element and can be used to attach plugins, retrieve additional data, and so on.

> Angular provides multiple ways to handle Dependency Injection, but two are the most common. In many examples, you'll see factory functions that look like `function($scope, $http) { ... }`, which works because Angular will actually inspect the variable names to determine what providers it should use, then inject those into the function, so `$scope` gets populated with an instance of the current scope, and `$http` gets the singleton instance of Angular's `$http` library. This is awesome, until you try minimizing your code, because once the variable names change, everything breaks. With that in mind, I recommend using the second approach, which requires passing in an array in place of the factory function, as we did earlier. In this case, you explicitly name what instances you need (`api` in our case, these can be our own custom services/filters in addition to those built into Angular), and then the last element in your array is the factory function itself, and each variable will be populated in the same order as your original array elements. This is the method I'll use throughout this book, and the one I recommend anytime you're writing code that you'll want to use in a production environment.

Naming

Naming of directives within Angular is pretty flexible, with a few conventions implemented to ensure consistency. All directives are named using camelCase in JavaScript, and snake case within your HTML. Snake case, here, means all lower case, using either `:`, `-`, or `_` to separate the words. Thus, for us, the JavaScript name `myAwesomeDirective` becomes `my-awesome-directive`, `my:awesome:directive`, or `my_awesome_directive` in the HTML, all of which will properly bind the directive to the DOM node. And finally, if you're running your HTML through a validator and don't like seeing warnings about each of your custom directives, you can even prepend `x-` or `data-` to the directive name and Angular will still detect it.

Attachment styles

No, we're not talking about relationships here. Directives can be invoked from within your HTML in multiple ways, though it's up to the developer to decide which ones they will allow. When developing your own directive, you can control which methods you want to utilize through the `restrict` property, using a subset of **EACM** (standing for element, attribute, class, comment).

By far, the most common method for invoking a directive is through an **attribute**, in large part because it's the default if the `restrict` property is left undefined. It's the method you've seen me use so far in all the examples, and outside of this section, all other examples we'll use this method as well. Declaring a directive via an attribute protects you from the issues we'll see shortly with Internet Explorer, and still provides a semantic indication within your HTML that you are declaring the function or nature of this node. For a quick reminder, here's what the attribute method looks like:

```
<div my-awesome-directive="something"></div>
```

The next method that you're likely to see is using the directive name as the **element name** itself.

```
<my-awesome-directive></my-awesome-directive>
```

This method has the advantage of being exceptionally semantically accurate, and, let's be honest, it looks the coolest because we're creating our own HTML elements. The disadvantage, as usual, is that Internet Explorer will read these in as `div` instances, thus preventing Angular from knowing that they even exist. You can get around this by using `document.createElement('my-awesome-directive')` in the head of your HTML, but you have to do this separately for each directive, and except in rare cases I usually consider it to be more work than it's worth.

The final two methods are **classname** and **comment**. Both are very rarely used, although I do know some developers who prefer using comments because they feel it keeps their HTML cleaner.

```
//As a class
<div class="my-awesome-directive: something;"></div>
//As an HTML comment
<!-- directive: my-awesome-directive something -->
```

Which method out of the four you use is almost entirely a matter of preference, though conventions do lean toward attributes, and most directives you use from other developers will likely at least support that method, if not use it exclusively.

Configuration options

Now that we have a good basis for how to create a blank directive and attach it to our DOM, let's take a look through the directive definition object, which is the official name for the object returned from the directive factory function. Remember that there are two ways to initialize a directive within the factory function. The first is to return our linking function, as we did earlier, and the second is to use this definition object to provide more fine-grained control over the way our directive functions. Using the definition object, our directive with all the options enumerated looks like the following code:

```
angular.module('myApp.directives', [])
.directive('myAwesomeDirective', ['api', function(api) {
  //Do any one-time directive initialization work here
  return {
    priority : 10,
    terminal : false,
    template: '<div><h3>{{title}}</h3></div>',
    templateUrl : 'myDirective.html',
    replace : true,
    compile : function (element, attributes, transclude) {},
    link : function ($scope, $element, $attrs) {},
    scope : true,
    controller : function ($scope, $element, $attrs) {},
    require : 'myAwesomeDirective',
    transclude : true
  };
}]);
```

Obviously you'll never use all of these options at the same time, however, let's dive into each one individually.

Priority

The first property we will look at is the `priority` option, which allows us to specify in what order directives should be executed, if there are multiple directives on the same node. The default is 0, and unlike many languages, higher numbers go first here. There is no specification for what order directives of the same priority will execute in, so if order is really important, it's best to make that explicit.

For simple tasks like attaching some data or initializing a jQuery plugin on your element, this option won't be necessary, however if your directive needs to modify the DOM in any way, particularly if it needs to add in other directives conditionally, you'll find this option exceptionally helpful.

Terminal

Closely tied to `priority`, `terminal` dictates whether or not directive execution should stop after the `priority` level. It's important to note, however, that this does not necessarily mean stop after this directive itself. Because the execution order of directives on the same priority level is not specified, directive processing continues after a terminal directive until the end of its priority level, ensuring that the results will be consistent. Like `priority`, this option is most useful in cases where conditional DOM manipulation is needed, something we'll study in greater detail in the next chapter.

Templating

If your directive provides a custom HTML structure, you can use the `template` or `templateUrl` property to define it. These templates can also contain other directives nested within them, and those will be initialized and attached as part of your directive's compilation process as well. Both template properties function largely in the same way, replacing the element's HTML with the specified template, although `template` takes an inline string, whereas `templateUrl` loads the HTML from an external file. Do note that the compile/link process for this directive will be suspended until the template is loaded, so if your custom HTML is minimal, it's usually more efficient to provide it inline.

Replace

Use of the `replace` property specifies whether the whole element should be replaced with the template, or if the template HTML should just replace the element's inner HTML. If you do choose to replace the entire element, note that Angular will do its best to copy over all of the classes/attributes from the original element, including merging the class attributes together. Additionally, if you want to replace the original element, your template must have only one root node. If you try to use a template with multiple root nodes (such as `<h2>{{title}}</h2><div>{{content}}</div>`), Angular will throw an error as there's no way to migrate the attributes over consistently.

Compiling and linking

The `compile` and `link` properties do the bulk of the DOM manipulation and the plugin binding work. We'll spend all of the next chapter discussing why the process is split into two parts like this, and when to use each. For the sake of an introduction, and as a massive over-simplification, you can think of `compile` as performing any tasks that require restructuring the DOM (and possibly adding other directives) regardless of the specific `scope`, and the `link` function as attaching a scope to that compiled element.

Remember that we said you could return a function directly from the factory function, instead of using this definition object? That function that we return is actually the link function discussed here, and is simply a shortcut to returning a definition object with only link defined.

One last important note on these properties, and then we'll save the rest for the next chapter. If you set a value for the compile property, Angular will ignore the link property. If you need to use both, you can return an object from the compile function, with pre set to your compile function, and post set to your link function, as demonstrated in the following code:.

```
angular.directive('myAwesomeDirective', function () {
    return {
    compile : function (tElement, tAttrs, transclude) {
      pre : function compile ($scope, $element, $attrs) {},
      post : function link ($scope, $element, $attrs) {}
      return{
      ...//current pre and post text
      }
    }
  }
});
```

Scope

As mentioned in *Chapter 2*, *The Need for Directives*, scoping with directives is one of the most powerful, yet confusing features of Angular, so we've dedicated all of *Chapter 5*, *Keeping it Clean with Scope*, to it. For now, let's just take a quick look at the three types of values the scope option can have.

If left undefined, the scope value is null, which tells Angular to give the directive the same scope as the object its attached to. This is by far the most common case, and is perfect for adding a few new values to watch as we did in the previous chapter. If, however, you want to generate a new scope for your directive, there are two ways you can do so.

First, simply set the scope parameter to true, which will create a new scope for the directive, but still inherit from it's parent. This means you'll still be able to read all of the values from your parent scope, including adding any new watchers to monitor data changes, but new values you write onto the scope won't affect the parent scope's values.

Note, this is a bit of an over generalization, as it's simply inherited from it's parent prototypically, like all other JavaScript objects. Which means if you set `$scope.name = "bob"` on the child scope, the parent won't be touched. If instead, however, you set `$scope.data.name = "bob"`, it will be changed, as you're actually reading the "data" object first, then setting the value on that, and since that object is shared between parent and child, both will reflect the change.

```
$scope.name = "bob"
$scope.data.name = "bob"
"data"
```

Secondly, if you want to isolate your directive from the rest of your application, you can create an aptly named **isolate scope**. This scope can be helpful in ensuring modularity and preventing accidental changes to data outside of your directive caused by shared properties or methods.

To create an isolate scope, simply pass in an object hash to the scope parameter. If it's empty, no values will be inherited and your scope will be completely isolated. You can also specify specific properties and attributes that you want to maintain access to, which we'll explore in *Chapter 5, Keeping it Clean with Scope*.

As a final note on scope for this chapter, each DOM element can only have one scope applied to it, which means that if you set `scope : true` for multiple directives on the same node, they'll all share the same new scope. While this is usually fine, do note that only one directive on a node can request an isolate scope, and all other directives will share that scope, so be careful with declaring an isolated scope too often, particularly if you intend to share this module with other developers who might need to isolate their own directives as well.

Controllers

The next two properties, `controller` and `require`, are closely related, so we'll look at them together. The `controller` function can store many of the same properties or methods that you might normally attach to the scope discussed earlier, however, if they are attached to the controller itself, they can be shared with other directives in the DOM tree. This sharing is done via the `require` property, which tells Angular to grab the instance of one directive's controller and make it available to another directive. As with much of Angular, this is somewhat complex to discuss in text, so let's take a look at an example of requiring an instance of `ngModel`, one of the most common controllers you'll request, as it's the basis for all two-way data binding. To start, here's the basic directive definition:

```
angular.directive('autocompleteInput', function () {
  return {
    require : 'ngModel',
    link : function ($scope, $element, $attrs, ngModel) {
      ngModel.$render = function () {
        $element.val(ngModel.$viewValue || '');
      };
      $element.autocomplete({
        ... //Define source, etc
        select : function (ev, ui) {
          $scope.$apply(function() {
            ngModel.$setViewValue(ui.item.value);
          });
        }
      });
    }
  }
});
```

Here we have an example of a simple directive that attaches the jQueryUI autocomplete plugin to an input, and handles updating the model when a selection is made. You can see we've used the `require` property to tell Angular that we want access to the controller instance on the `ngModel` directive, which then gets passed into our link function as the fourth parameter. Because we've required the `ngModel` controller, we also have to declare the directive that provides that controller, otherwise Angular will throw an error, which means that our input element needs to look something like this:

```
<input ng-model="data.property" autocomplete-input />
```

Obviously, throwing an error is often not what we want to happen, so Angular allows you to prepend a question mark, such as `?ngModel`, to make that requirement optional. You can also use a caret (`^ngModel`), to tell Angular to traverse upwards from the element node through the DOM tree and look for the directive in the elements there, such as the following:

```
<div ng-model="data.property">
  <input autocomplete-input />
</div>
```

The `ngModel` controller provides multiple methods and properties, but for our purposes we only need two, `$render` and `$setViewValue()`. The `ngModel` directive calls `$render` whenever the value of the data element that it's bound to (`data.property` in the preceding code) changes. Thus, once we assign our custom function to the `$render` key, any time the data changes, we can update the input value appropriately. `$setViewValue` works in the opposite direction, so when the user does something that should change the value, we can tell `ngModel` what the new value is and it will update the internal data model.

If you need access to multiple controllers, you can also pass in an array to the `require` property, and likewise the fourth parameter of your `link` function will be an array of those controllers.

Defining your own controller is a bit outside the scope of this chapter, so we'll revisit that later in *Chapter 6, Controllers – Better with Sharing*.

Transclusion

Just like the previous few sections, the `transclude` property deserves its own chapter, and so we'll explore it more in *Chapter 7, Transclusion*. In short, transclusion provides the ability to have an isolate scope as we discussed earlier, and still have access to the parent scope's properties for internal content. If that doesn't make any sense, that's normal, even the developers of Angular themselves concede that:

> *This may seem to be a unexpected complexity, but it gives the widget user and the developer the least surprise.*

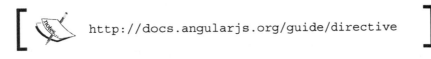

```
http://docs.angularjs.org/guide/directive
```

While indeed providing helpful functionality, for most directives, transclusion is simply too much complexity for what we need, and thus we're going to leave it alone until *Chapter 7, Transclusion*. By that point, you'll hopefully be more comfortable with the more core attributes of directives.

Summary

Hopefully by this point I've whetted your appetite by elaborating on some of the power that each directive can utilize. The simpler properties such as template, priority, and basic linking should already have demonstrated a taste of the kind of modular extensibility directives can add to your development arsenal. And we'll revisit each of these properties over the next several chapters as we dive into the inner workings of scoping, controllers, and transclusion, as I recognize many of the options discussed likely still seem like a magic black box. Next, however, let's take a look at some of Angular's built in directives, `ng-repeat` and `ng-switch`, for a study into why we separate `compile` and `link`, and how you can use that for your own custom directives as well.

4
Compile versus Link

Within Angular directives, there are two primary phases that handle the process of connecting the directive logic to the DOM, as well as performing any necessary DOM manipulation. The first phase is the **compile phase**, which works on the element before it's been inserted into the document, and thus is great for performance, but can't be used to attach any DOM related plugins since the element isn't accessible yet. The second phase is the **linking** phase, which works on the element after it has been inserted into the DOM and has the appropriate scope instance created and initialized for it. For this chapter, we'll start by reviewing a couple directives built into Angular as an example of why this separation exists and how it can best be used, and then we'll create a few of our own examples to explore it in more detail.

Peeking under the covers

Let's first take a quick look at what Angular actually does with the functions it receives from the compile and link properties, and how they're used during the full compilation process. The first thing to know is that both returning a function from our directive factory (instead of using the definition object) and defining a function on the link parameter are really just shortcuts to setting the compile property to be a function that returns that same linking function. In other words, no matter how we define our link function, by the time Angular gets around to processing our directive, it will always call the compile function and take what it returns as the linking function(s). For proof, here are few lines of code that make that initial call:

```
...
linkFn = directive.compile($compileNode, templateAttrs,
  childTranscludeFn);
  if (isFunction(linkFn)) {
    addLinkFns(null, linkFn);
    //Only attach to 'postLink' functions
    }else if (linkFn) {
    addLinkFns(linkFn.pre, linkFn.post);
  }
```

There are a couple of important things to note from this code before we move on. First, compile is called really early on during this whole process. $compileNode represents the element we're manipulating, but it's not anywhere in the DOM just yet, instead it's much like what you would receive if you called jQuery (<div>). What this means is while we can manipulate it within the compile function (and if we need to conditionally add other directives or change the pre-parsed HTML, this is where we have to manipulate it), we can't attach any DOM listeners or plugins that need to process a fully-realized node just yet. Secondly, there are actually two types of linking functions, pre and post. When Angular is processing your directive, it will first execute any and all of the pre-linking functions on the directive element itself, then it will recurse down into any child nodes within the element and compile those, then walk back up the DOM tree and execute all of the post-linking functions. As a result, the whole compilation process proceeds through the following flow:

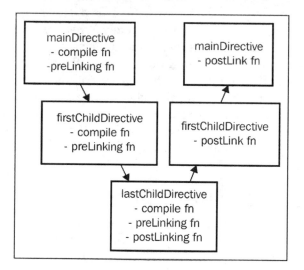

As a general rule, the same DOM manipulation restrictions apply to both the compile function and the pre-linking function, since the element is still being updated by Angular and cannot be cloned or otherwise modified before creating the final instance that will be inserted into the document. The post-linking function, on the other hand, receives the final element and can be manipulated as you need. The majority of your directives will likely just use the post-linking function. The pre-linking function is only advantageous when you need to perform some individualized preparation on the scope or controller object before any child elements compile, so we'll review that use case in more detail in *Chapter 6, Controllers–Better with Sharing*. Compile, on the other hand, is ideal when you need to make use of the transclusion function or conditionally modify your element before it's compiled, so we'll review a couple use cases of that in this chapter.

ng-repeat

To start our study into the primary use cases for the compile function, let's take a look at the definition object for the built-in directive `ng-repeat`. The definition object is as follows:

```
...
.directive('ngRepeat', function () {
  return {
    priority: 1000,
    transclude: 'element',
    terminal: true,
    compile: function(element, attr, linker) { // Compile Function
      return function(scope, iterStartElement, attr){ // Linking
Function
      };
    }
  }
});
```

The first few properties should be familiar from the previous chapter, but let's quickly review how each is used here. A `priority` value of 1000 makes sure that this directive executes before any others on the element, and setting `terminal` to true ensures that Angular's automatic compilation doesn't continue on to any other directives on this element or its children. We want this because the `ng-repeat` compile function itself will actually be handling the compilation processing for the node tree of child elements. A `transclude` value of `element` is used to collect the HTML content of the original element, as we'll need that to be able to compile it later and as such we'll see that it is used here shortly within the compile function.

Compile

The compile function declared in the preceding section takes three properties. The first is the template element, meaning it contains all the HTML within our DOM node, but again, this doesn't necessarily represent the instance of that element that's actually going to be inserted into our final document. The second property is similar to the `$attrs` object that was passed to our linking function in *Chapter 3, Deconstructing Directives*. It contains normalized access to each attribute on the DOM element. Remember, however, that we don't have an initialized scope here, so any of the attribute values that need to be evaluated within a scope won't have a useful value yet.

For the purpose of our examination, however, the final parameter is by far the most valuable. This `linker` is the transcluded function, which Angular would normally use to attach a scope to this element, interpolate all of the values, and then insert the final object into the DOM. By grabbing this linking function, `ng-repeat` now has control over when to perform the actual linking, as well as the ability to repeatedly do so, which of course is exactly what we need.

Link

The linking function is what the compile function returns. Because, in the case of `ng-repeat`, we only need to get access to the transcluding function, and not actually do any DOM manipulation on the template element, we can just return that immediately.

At the heart of the `ng-repeat` linking function is `$scope.$watch`, which serves to connect the data and data changes to the rest of our code. As a quick note of introduction, the `$watch` method's first argument can take two types of parameters. The first type is a simple string that corresponds to a scoped variable and is evaluated against the current scope; this is the method you'll probably use most commonly. The second type is a full function which takes the current scope as its own first parameter and allows for more complex comparisons. In both cases, any time the `return` value changes or is first initialized, the function passed in to `$watch` as the second parameter is called. In our case here of `ng-repeat`, we're actually using the `watcher` function (first parameter) to perform all of the necessary changes, since it gets called every time Angular executes the `$digest` function. As a note, I wouldn't actually recommend this method unless you're confident it's necessary and you've extensively optimized your `watcher` function, as this can get called several times a second.

The actual internals of the `$watcher` function are more complicated than it is worthwhile for us to dive into for the goals of this chapter, so we'll operate off this simplified model for the purpose of our discussion.

```
compile: function (element, attrs, linker) {
  return function ($scope, $element, $attrs) { // "post" Linking
function
    $scope.$watch(function ($internalScope) {
```

```
    $element.html('');// Clear the element's current HTML
    var values = ... // Read in array to iterate over
    values.forEach(function (data, index) {
        $internalScope.element = data; // Attach this element's data
properties to the 'element' property on the scope so we can use it
within the template
        linker($internalScope, function (clone) {
            $element.append(clone); // Take the interpolated HTML and
append it to our main $element
        }); // end of linker clone function
    }); // end of forEach
  }); // end of $watch
}; // end of linking function
} // end of compile function
```

Obviously, we're setting aside some necessary caching and sorting methods, however for our purposes this represents the key process. We begin by reading in the current values for our array, iterating over each element to assign it to our scope, and then performing magic.

Well, almost magic. We're finally going to use that `linker` function we've been working up to for this whole section. Remember that we fetched this from the compile property, which means it's imbued with all of the requisite knowledge of our directive template (if there is one), the internal HTML within our element node, and is all but salivating at the chance to show off its skills at scope binding and interpolation. And since it's never wise to disappoint an anxious function, we're finally going to oblige it by sending in our newly crafted scope, along with a secondary function to handle the result.

Within the `linker` function, the scope gets bound to the compiled, but not yet interpolated, element HTML, and a new "fully transformed" element is generated. That element gets passed to our secondary function as the `clone` parameter, whereby we use a little standard jQuery DOM manipulation to insert our `clone` element into the DOM at the end of our original element.

In a (somewhat large) nutshell, that's how `ng-repeat` makes use of the compile property to transform an element DOM structure, not just once, but continuously as the data changes. Now let's continue and check out `ng-switch`, another built-in directive that makes use of the compile property, though in a slightly different way.

ng-switch

Since we've already covered attaching directives extensively, we're not going to examine the HTML of an ng-switch directive in detail. However, in the interest of having a reference point while going through the JavaScript, here's a simple example shown in the following code snippet:

```html
<div ng-switch="currentSport">
  <p ng-switch-when="baseball">Home run!</p>
  <p ng-switch-when="football">Touchdown!</p>
  <p ng-switch-default>Goal!</p>
</div>
```

For an unexpected twist in the story, let's take a look at the ng-switch definition object:

```javascript
{
  restrict: 'EA',
  require: 'ngSwitch',
  controller: function () {
    this.cases = {};
  },
  link: function(scope, element, attr, ctrl) {
    var watchExpr = attr.ngSwitch, // Read in the data property we
want to monitor
        selectedLinker,
        selectedElement,
        selectedScope;
    scope.$watch(watchExpr, function (value) {
      if (selectedElement) { // remove any prior HTML within $element
        selectedScope.$destroy();
        selectedElement.remove();
        selectedElement = selectedScope = null;
      }
      if ((selectedLinker = ctrl.cases['!' + value] || ctrl.
cases['?'])) {
        selectedScope = scope.$new();
        selectedLinker(selectedScope, function(caseElement) {
          selectedElement = caseElement;
          element.append(caseElement);
        });
      }
    });
  }
}
```

I warned you there was a twist, and you've likely already seen it... there's no compile property here. That's right; our next foray into this study of compilation doesn't even include a compile property on the main directive. That's because ng-switch is actually a collection of three different directives, all of which work together, and it's on these other two directives that compile makes its shining appearance.

The two supplemental directives, ng-switch-when and ng-switch-default, work in nearly the same way, and function just as you might expect if you have any experience with switch statements in other languages. ng-switch-when serves to match against a specific case, and display its associated element if a match is made. On the other hand, ng-switch-default comes into play if no matches can be found. Because they're so similar, we'll only look in depth at the code of ng-switch-when, but I'll point out the one place they differ just so you can have a fuller understanding of it. Without further ado, let's have a look at the following ng-switch-when directive:

```
{
  transclude: 'element',
  priority: 500,
  require: '^ngSwitch',
  compile: function(element, attrs, linker) {
    return function(scope, element, attr, ctrl) {
      // For ng-switch-default, the linker function is simply attached
to the '?' key within ctrl.cases
      ctrl.cases['!' + attrs.ngSwitchWhen] = linker;
    };
  }
}
```

In the same manner as we just saw with ng-repeat, we're once again setting the transclude property to element in order to request an instance of the linking function. This time, however, we've also grabbed an instance of the ngSwitch controller. We'll talk more about controllers in *Chapter 6, Controllers–Better with Sharing*, but for now just remember that when we request a controller with require, we're fetching the same instance that's in use on the ng-switch directive itself, and thus is shared with ng-switch and all of the other ng-switch-[when/default] directives as well.

Unlike ng-repeat, we're not going to use the linker function immediately, but instead we use the subordinate directives (when/default) to collect all of the possible linker functions, and thus their respective DOM elements, and then store them on the primary ng-switch controller for use there. Once again, we use $watch to connect the data to our code, though in this case we're using the more common string method. This time, instead of grabbing a specific data element to update our scope, we're grabbing the transclude function that's attached to a particular template, allowing us to update the element HTML automatically to reflect changes in the data.

What about linking?

Ok, so now that we've taken a look at some of the uses for compile, you may be wondering when you would ever want to use link. The answer: pretty much always. First of all, realize that both of the examples we reviewed in the preceding section use the linking function; they just initialize it differently, then return it from the compile function instead of attaching it directly to the `link` property. Secondly, while the ability to have low level access to the element template and fine-tune exactly when and where the `linker` function comes into play sounds awesome (and it is), in reality there are actually very few times you'll need that much control. Out of the 26 different directives included with the awesome AngularUI library, only three use the compile property. And even those primarily use the compile function simply for validating the directive options and prepping variables so they don't have to be repeatedly looked up.

Summary

So, in the end, the compile function is awesome. It's also rarely needed. Most of the time, your `link` function will handle all of the heavy lifting for you, and adding in the compile option just creates unnecessary complexity within your code. On the other hand, when you need to be able to manipulate the template element before binding to the scope, or want to conditionally apply the `linker` function as the data changes, compile offers you that option. Next chapter we'll dive into scoping, a helpful way to ensure your data is properly linked, yet still modular, both inside and outside your directives.

5

Keeping it Clean with Scope

"Why do we [scope], Master Wayne? So we can [stay modular and code like a rockstar]"

> \- Alfred (if he'd been an Angular developer)

As you've likely seen so far, the scope object within Angular serves as the primary intersection point between our data, our view, and the rest of our code. Any property or method that's available on our scope can be accessed and used within our HTML. Likewise, any changes that happen to the data will update the HTML and can trigger other updates within the rest of code, via the `$watch` method that we've already used several times.

Those qualities of scope pervade nearly all of Angular development. Within a directive however, scoping takes on an even more powerful role, allowing us to plug directly into the rest of the application scope, remain completely separate, or utilize some blend of both.

> As a quick reminder about scoping when there are multiple directives on an element, all directives receive the same scope, and whichever directive requests the most limited scope gets priority. This means that a scope of "true" trumps a scope of "false", and an isolate scope (object hash) trumps them all.

Now, with whetted appetite, let's take a look at the three types of values we can use: **false**, **true**, and an **object hash**.

Scope = false

A scope property value of false is the default for all directive definition objects. If you've done much Angular development before, you might be tempted to assume that this operates in the same manner as nesting another controller, where each directive gets a new inherited scope. With directives, however, that's actually not the case. When a new directive is initialized with a scope property of false, that directive receives the same scope as its parent. Not an inherited scope, but the exact same object. This means that all changes to the parent scope will be reflected within our directive, and also any change within our directive's scope will be reflected within the parent.

To help explain the unique characteristics of this and the other types of scoping, take a look at the following HTML and directive declaration:

```
<div ng-init="title = 'Hello World'">
  <h2 id="appTitle">{{title}}</h2>
  <button id="newAppTitle" ng-click="setAppTitle('App 2.0')">Upgrade
me!</button>
  <div my-scoped-directive>
    <h4 id="directiveTitle">{{title}}</h4>
    <button id="newDirTitle" ng-click="setDirectiveTitle('bob')">Bob
it!</button>
  </div>
</div>
...
directive('myScopedDirective', function() {
  return {
    scope : false, // we could leave this out, since it's the default
    link : function ($scope, $element, $attrs) {
      $scope.setDirectiveTitle = function (title) {
        $scope.title = title;
      };
    }
  };
});
```

To help visualize what happens here, let's diagram the effects of compilation and user interaction on our $parentScope and $directiveScope:

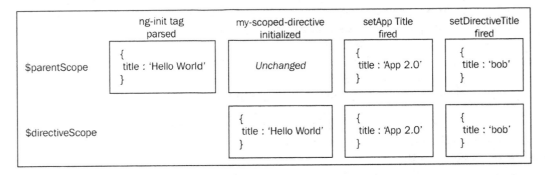

	ng-init tag parsed	my-scoped-directive initialized	setApp Title fired	setDirectiveTitle fired

$parentScope	{
	title : 'Hello World'
	}
		Unchanged	{
			title : 'App 2.0'
			}
				{
				title : 'bob'
				}

$directiveScope		{
		title : 'Hello World'
		}
			{
			title : 'App 2.0'
			}
				{
				title : 'bob'
				}

As you can see, when Angular first parses through this HTML, it sees the ng-init attribute, which it evaluates within the current scope before proceeding, and thus sets $scope.title equal to Hello World. Then, when the element is fully compiled and linked, both #appTitle and #directiveTitle will say Hello World. We developers are curious, however, which means that if there's a button, we must click it. When we click the #newDirTitle button, the setDirectiveTitle method gets called and, working directly on our directive's scope, sets $scope.title to now say bob. You might expect at this point #appTitle to still read Hello World and #directiveTitle to bob. Remember however, that because we've set scope to false, the parent scope and the directive scope are in fact the same object, and thus both #appTitle and #directiveTitle will now read bob.

Sometimes, this behavior is exactly what we want. Setting the scope to false gives us unbridled interconnectivity with the parent scope and thus the rest of our application. Such power, however, comes with a price. As you can see in the preceding paragraph, it is exceptionally easy to accidentally change data in the rest of your application when using a non-scoped directive and so, unless you're sure you need that much connectedness, my recommendation is to use a more limited scope whenever possible.

Scope = true

The first step down the path of limiting, or modularizing, your scope is setting its value to `true`. In this case, a new inherited scope is actually generated, much like the behavior when nesting controllers. This type of scoping for a directive is by far the easiest to understand and operate within, as you still have read access to all of the parent scope's values, but it's less likely that you'll accidentally change the data in the rest of the application. For this reason, I usually recommend setting scope to `true` from the beginning, unless you have a strong reason to do otherwise.

To help clarify the difference of this type of scoping, let's revisit our previous example. This time, the scope section of our definition object will be `scope: true`, but otherwise all of the code will remain the same. When we first load the page, this directive will be indistinguishable from our previously false-scoped directive; both `#appTitle` and `#directiveTitle` will still say `Hello World` because our directive's scope is inherited from the parent.

We discussed this inheritance briefly earlier, but as a reminder, this is the prototypical inheritance innate to JavaScript. As such, any value not explicitly declared on our scope will be read from the parent, or parent's parent, all the way up to `$rootScope`. The caveat, of course, is that setting, or writing, values does not work that same way. As soon as we set a value, it's stored locally and we lose all connection to any ancestral property of the same name. Again, let's see how our directive will flow given our newly updated scope parameter, as shown in the following figure:

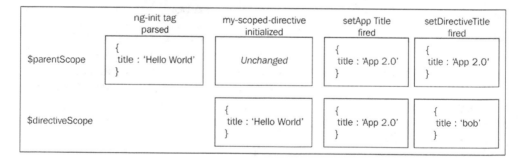

	ng-init tag parsed	my-scoped-directive initialized	setApp Title fired	setDirectiveTitle fired

$parentScope	{
	title : 'Hello World'
	}
		Unchanged	{
			title : 'App 2.0'
			}
				{
				title : 'App 2.0'
				}

$directiveScope		{
		title : 'Hello World'
		}
			{
			title : 'App 2.0'
			}
				{
				title : 'bob'
				}

As you can see, what this new scope object means for us is that once we click on our button and fire `setDirectiveTitle`, `#directiveTitle` will change to `bob`, however `#appTitle` will still say `Hello World`. This type of scoping has all of the advantages and disadvantages of prototypical inheritance. We get to keep read access to the rest of the application's data, and even the updates to it, as demonstrated by our firing of `setAppTitle`, without having to worry about accidentally overwriting anything. On the other hand, for values that you do want to change, it does require keeping track of which values are local and which are inherited, as well as using inherited methods to change any ancestral values.

Scope = {}

For times when you want to have complete control over which properties and methods are interconnected within your new directive scope, an object hash is usually your best solution. This type of scoping is commonly referred to as an **isolate scope**, because of the lack of connectedness with the other scopes within the application. An empty object signifies that you want the new scope to be completely isolated from its parents, so nothing is inherited or carried over. If absolutely necessary, you can still access the parent or root scopes by using the $parent and $root properties, respectively, however this goes directly against our goals of modularity and thus should only be used when there's no better option.

While there are a few instances where we want our directive to be entirely isolated, more commonly we'll want to maintain access to a few explicitly specified properties and methods from the ancestral scope tree. To do this, Angular provides three symbols for notating what type of access you want to acquire: @, =, and &, which are prepended to the attribute names that you want to derive a value from. As such, we can create an isolate scope that looks like this:

```
scope : {
  'myReadonlyVariable' : '@myStringAttr',
  'myTwowayVariable' : '=myParentProperty',
  'myInternalFunction' : '&myParentFunction'
}
```

@ – read-only Access

Using the @ symbol to retrieve a value from your attributes means that the attribute value will be interpolated and whatever is returned will be stored within the scope property that you specify. To help explain, let's expand our previous scoping example with a few extra details as shown in the following code snippet:

```
<div ng-init="title = 'Hello World'">
  <h2 id="appTitle">{{title}}</h2>
  <button id="newAppTitle" ng-click="setAppTitle('App 2.0')">Upgrade
me!</button>
  <div my-scoped-directive msd-title="I'm a directive, within the app
{{title}}">
    <h4 id="directiveTitle">{{title}}</h4>
    <button id="newDirTitle" ng-click="setDirectiveTitle('bob')">Bob
it!</button>
  </div>
</div>
...
```

```
directive('myScopedDirective', function() {
  return {
    scope : {
      'title' : '@msdTitle'
    },
    link : function ($scope, $element, $attrs) {
      $scope.setDirectiveTitle = function (title) {
        $scope.title = title;
      };
    }
  };
});
```

First, as a quick reminder, within our JavaScript, all attribute names are normalized to be camelCased, which is why we refer to the HTML attribute `msd-title` as `msdTitle` within our scoping object. Secondly, take note of how our attribute string is evaluated. The `{{title}}` value in our attribute will be evaluated within the parent scope, not in the new internal scope we're creating. Thus, in this example, `#appTitle` will still be `Hello World`, but `#directiveTitle` will now read `I'm a directive, within the app Hello World`.

Thirdly, it is important to realize that even though we've requested only read-only access for this attribute, it will still be dynamically updated when the parent scope changes. If a user clicks on our `#setAppTitle` button, the `#appTitle` will be updated to `App 2.0` and `#directiveTitle` will mirror that change by now reading `I'm a directive, within the app App 2.0`.

Of course, as you can probably ascertain by the "read-only" nature of this access, the reverse is not true. If our user now clicks on our `#setDirTitle` button, `#appTitle` will remain unchanged, `#directiveTitle` will now read `bob`, and, most importantly, we've now severed the connection between the two values. The following figure provides insight into the state of our data at each point of the process:

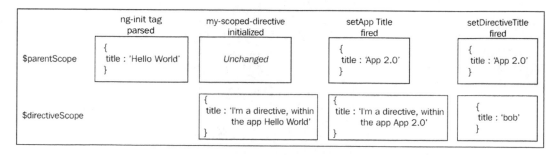

From this point forward, any updates to the parent scope's title property will be ignored by our directive, as we've overridden our original linked value with a new static value. If we you need both read and write access to a property, you will need to instead utilize the following method for requesting property access.

= – two-way binding

For occasions where you want full access to a specific property on the parent scope, Angular provides the = symbol for use within our isolate scope. Let's extend our original example again to see how this can be useful:

```
<div ng-init="title = 'Hello World'; subtitle = 'I am an app'">
  <h2 id="appTitle">{{title}}</h2>
  <h3 id="appSub">{{subtitle}}</h3>
  <button id="newAppTitle" ng-click="setAppTitle('App 2.0')">Upgrade
me!</button>
  <div my-scoped-directive msd-title="I'm a directive, within the app
{{title}}" msd-subtitle="subtitle">
    <h4 id="directiveTitle">{{title}}</h4>
    <button id="newDirTitle" ng-click="setDirectiveTitle('bob')">Bob
it!</button>
    <button id="newDirSub" ng-click="setDirectiveSubtitle('Time to
submerge')">Empty the ballasts!</button>
  </div>
</div>
directive('myScopedDirective', function() {
  return {
    scope : {
      'title' : '@msdTitle',
      'subtitle' : '=msdSubtitle'
    },
    link : function ($scope, $element, $attrs) {
      $scope.setDirectiveTitle = function (title) {
        $scope.title = title;
      };
      $scope.setDirectiveSubtitle = function (subtitle) {
        $scope.subtitle = subtitle;
      };
    }
  };
});
```

Now that's we've updated our code, the data model now proceeds through the following flow:

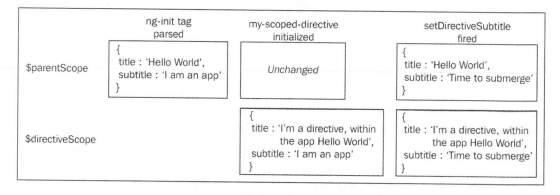

Within this scenario, our `subtitle` property works in exactly the same way as it would if we had set the entire scope property to `false`. When our app is first initialized, both subtitles will read `I am an app`. If we fire the `setDirectiveSubtitle` method, however, both values will again change, this time reading `Time to submerge`. Given that this method of binding is identical to a false scope property, we might be inclined to wonder why this option is even provided. The difference here is that we only have this two-way binding for properties that we explicitly specify, which helps us ensure modularity. Because of the way we've bound our property, we don't care about the name of our parent property. It could be `lesser-title-the-third` for all we care, and as long as that property is passed into our `msd-subtitle` attribute, our directive will continue to function in exactly the same way, including updating the parent scope's property when our button is clicked. And, of course, the reverse is also true. When developing our parent application, we don't need to worry about our property names conflicting with those used in our directive and suddenly being overwritten. This type of binding plays a huge role in making sure a directive can be plugged into any application and have both the directive and the application function as their respective developers intended.

& – method binding

Sometimes, however, it's not simply properties that you want to be able to maintain access to. Sometimes you need to be able to call a method on the parent scope. For this, the symbol of choice is &, and let's once again return to our example to see how this symbol is used, as shown in the following code snippet:

```
<div ng-init="title = 'Hello World'; subtitle = 'I am an app'">
  <h2 id="appTitle">{{title}}</h2>
  <h3 id="appSubtitle">{{subtitle}}</h3>
```

```
   <button id="upgradeApp" ng-click="setAppTitle('App 2.0', 'Still an
app')">Upgrade me!</button>
   <div my-scoped-directive msd-update-title="setAppTitle(title,
'Updated by a directive')">
      <h4 id="directiveTitle">{{title}}</h4>
      <button id="bobApp" ng-click="updateTitle({title : 'bob'})">Bob
it!</button>
   </div>
</div>
//Parent scope:
$scope.setAppTitle = function (title, subtitle) {
   $scope.title = title;
   $scope.subtitle = subtitle;
}
...
directive('myScopedDirective', function() {
   return {
      scope : {
         'updateTitle' : '&msdUpdateTitle'
      },
      link : function ($scope, $element, $attrs) {
         $scope.title = 'Lonely Directive';
      }
   };
});
```

Method binding is by far the most complicated of all scope bindings, so don't worry if it doesn't all make sense instantly. In most cases if you need to share methods between parent and child directives, I'd recommend using controllers (see our next chapter) whenever possible, however this is helpful if for some reason your method has to be scoped. Once more, the following diagram demonstrates the flow of the data model as our user interacts with our elements:

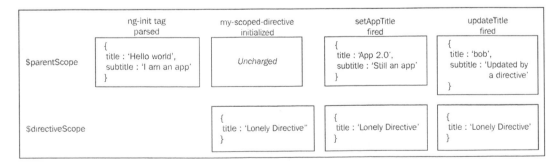

In this example, we've extended our parent scope's `setAppTitle` method to take two arguments, allowing us to update both the title and subtitle at the same time. We've also requested access to that same function and passed it in via the `msd-update-title` attribute. Note, however, that we don't just ask for it by name. Instead, the attribute value actually calls the function with a set of variable and/or hard-coded parameters. Then, within our new scope, Angular creates a wrapper function that takes a map of the variable names and values (the `{title : 'bob'}` parameter in our example) and calls our original method within the context of the parent scope, passing in all mapped values and other hard-coded parameters.

What this means is that when we first click on the `#upgradeApp` button, our `#appTitle` will become `App 2.0` and our `#appSubtitle` will read `Still an app`. If, however, we click on the `#bobApp` button within our directive, our wrapper function, bound to `updateTitle` within our directive's scope will be called, the `title` variable within our `msd-update-title` value will be mapped to `bob`, and finally `setAppTitle('bob','Updated by a directive')` will be called within the parent scope. It's important to emphasize that the entire function is called within the parent scope, so even though we're passing in a title value and calling it from the directive, it's the parent scope's title property that we're actually updating.

Again, binding a method like this is one of the most complex binding options Angular offers for use in an isolate scope, however it also allows you as the developer once again to remain fully modular, having to worry about the internal logic within the `setAppTitle` method, or even what it's called, and yet still be able to trigger it as you see fit. This type of access can be especially helpful when you want to be able to trigger a data refresh from an external source, but don't want your directive to know anything about how to go about that refresh or any data processing that needs to happen before or after the new content is received.

Summary

If you've made it this far, I trust you're convinced of the value of modularity and are interested in the ways Angular directives can make that easier for you. Scoping, particularly isolate scopes, is one of the most fundamental pieces of enabling that modularity. While the default scope value of **false** can certainly be convenient, and is often useful during early development and debugging, I strongly recommend not using it within your final production code unless you know it's absolutely necessary, and certainly not when you're developing a directive intended to be packaged and made available for use in other applications. The new scope provided by a value of **true** does provide a helpful compromise, though is still often more access than you need for a packaged directive. Hopefully by now, you see the value of an **isolate scope**, even though it does require some additional effort up front to consider all of the properties and methods you might need. If not, hold on, it'll demonstrate its usefulness even more in the coming chapters. In the next chapter, we'll be talking about controllers, and the ways they can be shared across multiple directives to extend the functionality of each.

6
Controllers – Better with Sharing

In *Chapter 4, Compile versus Link*, we walked through the compile and link steps of the Angular compilation process. What we set aside, at that point, were controllers, which are also functions that execute as Angular applies a directive. In and of themselves, controllers don't provide significant advantages over local methods within the linking function of your directives. When paired with their ability to be shared across directives, however, controllers provide unparalleled communication between directives on the same node, or even just within the same ancestral tree. To get a better understanding of how these controllers can enable directives to work together, let's take a look at the ngModel and form controllers, which combine to provide much of the real-time data binding that powers Angular's dynamic content.

Forms and inputs

Within Angular, every form element is also a directive whose primary purpose is to instantiate a FormController object, attach it to the form element and, if the form is named, register that form controller on the parent scope so that it can be more easily accessed. Likewise, all input and input-esque elements (for purposes of this discussion, we'll include the select and textarea tags within the input elements category) are also built-in directives, although unless they have an ng-model attribute on them, they don't actually have any extra functionality.

Our HTML for this example is pretty simple, just a simple form with a single input element.

```
<form name="exampleForm">
  <input type="text" ng-model="myName" />
</form>
```

The `FormController` function is primarily responsible for monitoring the overall validity of the form, based upon the validity of the individual elements within it. It does this through the use of the four main functions within the controller function outlined as shown:

```
function FormController(element, attrs) {
  //All controller functions and properties you want to export are
  bound to 'this'
  this.$addControl = function(control) { ...}; //Register an input
  element
  this.$removeControl = function(control) { ...}; //Unregister an
  element
  this.$setValidity = function(validationToken,
    isValid, control) { ...}; //Set the validity for a specific
  element
  this.$setDirty = function() {...}; //Mark the form as having been
  modified
}
```

For the purposes of this discussion, we're not going to worry about the internal logic of the `FormController` functions, what instead I want you to note is that, on its own, this controller does absolutely nothing. It's a handy collection of functions, but without any input elements, a form is simply sitting there, "valid", but otherwise unimpressive.

You've (hopefully) read the introductory paragraph, however, so you already knew that, and are now sitting there patiently waiting for the big reveal where `ngModelController` arises with a flourish and shows you just how cool controllers really are. Well, far be it from me to fool you twice (yes, I know after the whole `select` directive and compile twist, you might be cautious), so let's dive straight into the `ngModelController` function:

```
NgModelController = function($scope, $exceptionHandler, $attr,
$element, $parse) {
  this.$render = noop;
  var parentForm = $element.inheritedData('$formController') ||
nullFormCtrl;
```

```
   this.$setValidity = function(validationErrorKey, isValid) {
     ... //Internal processing
     parentForm.$setValidity(validationErrorKey, isValid, this);
   };
   this.$setViewValue = function(value) { ... };
};
```

And then finally, tying it all together is the ng-model directive, which grabs both controllers and teaches them to share:

```
ngModelDirective = function() {
  return {
    require: ['ngModel', '^form'],
    controller: NgModelController,
    link: function(scope, element, attr, ctrls) {
      var modelCtrl = ctrls[0], //grab the instance of the ngModel
controller
        formCtrl = ctrls[1]
      formCtrl.$addControl(modelCtrl);
      element.bind('$destroy', function() {
        formCtrl.$removeControl(modelCtrl);
      });
    }
  };
};
```

So yes, I admit, that was a lot of code. Feel free to go walk around the block to let it all settle in your mind before continuing... Ok, cool, let's dive in then. Part of the reason there's so much code is that that's what makes controllers powerful, they provide the ability to tie together large amounts of otherwise disconnected code into a cohesive package. In this example, you can see that when the ng-model directive initializes, it requests an array of controllers, both its own and the FormController, the latter of which is both optional and can be located on ancestral elements.

Let's go ahead and walk through the code to see how that all comes together. Remember that the compilation process proceeds down the DOM tree, so the FormController function initializes first. After the form is compiled, Angular works its way down to our input element, where it initializes the ngModelController function:

```
NgModelController = function($scope, $exceptionHandler, $attr,
$element, $parse) {
  this.$render = noop; //Each directive that requires ngModel must
implement this method to properly display the value
```

```
// Grab the form controller if there is one
var parentForm = $element.inheritedData('$formController') ||
nullFormCtrl;
this.$setValidity = function(validationErrorKey, isValid) {
  ... //Internal processing
  parentForm.$setValidity(validationErrorKey, isValid, this);
};
this.$setViewValue = function(value) { ... };
};
```

Before we continue, there are a couple of things to note here. First, unlike the link and compile functions, you can pass in any available service or dependency, such as $exceptionHandler and $parse in the preceding example. Additionally, we can grab the FormController function off the element data ($element.inheritedData('$formController')), which we can then use to pass validity information as part of each input's own $setValidity method. This connecting of controllers to elements all happens via the directive, and is our first example of using directive controllers to coordinate across elements.

Once the ngModelController function is initialized, Angular continues with the compilation process and triggers the linking function on the element itself, as shown in the following code:

```
ngModelDirective = function() {
  return {
    require: ['ngModel', '^form'],
//request an array of controllers. Look for formController on parent
elements
    controller: NgModelController,
    link: function(scope, element, attr, ctrls) {
      var modelCtrl = ctrls[0],
//grab the instance of the ngModel controller
        formCtrl = ctrls[1];
//grab the form controller
      formCtrl.$addControl(modelCtrl);
//register our ngModel controller

      element.bind('$destroy', function() {
        formCtrl.$removeControl(modelCtrl);
//unregister our controller if this element is removed
      });
    }
  };
};
```

As a reminder, the `require` property can be a string if we only want one controller, or an array as we have here. With the array format, the `ctrls` parameter passed into our linking function is also an array, in the same order as we requested them. Here, we've grabbed both controllers, and thus are able to call the `FormController`'s `addControl` method and pass in our `ngModelController` function. From this point forward, each controller, and therefore each directive, is fully aware of the relevant changes happening on the other.

At this point, you may be asking why we're not simply using basic messaging with `$broadcast` and `$emit` to communicate between our directives. There are two basic reasons why we prefer controllers over messaging in this scenario:

- First, idealistically, using controllers is significantly more modular. It allows us to separate out instance code that needs to be shared and available for cross-directive communication from the rest of the scope, while still keeping such methods available for convenient usage.

- Secondly, more pragmatically, controllers are far easier to utilize for scenarios like this. Messaging is designed primarily for a shotgun notification approach, such that when an event happens, you broadcast it to all of the elements above or below your current node, and then continue on. Controllers, however, allow for a much more targeted communication style, calling methods on specific nodes as necessary, and while we didn't use them here, also allowing for easy callback integration. Doing the same sort of targeted communication via messaging requires significant extra logic on the part of the listeners to determine whether or not they're the intended node.

There are certainly still plenty of times where the more open broadcast style of messaging suits your goals better. Controllers simply fill in when a more targeted approach is preferred.

Creating our own controller communication

Most likely, you'll find that `ngModel` is the most common controller you'll require within your code. Any time you want to create a custom input, or even just bind an input plugin that requires specific formatting, `ngModel` provides the methods you'll need to coordinate communication between the plugin and your data model.

With that in mind, let's walk through the process of creating an input for time values that utilizes the handy timepicker jQuery plugin provided by Jon Thornton. Our goal is to be able to turn a regular text field input into a timepicker that displays its value in the format HH:mm but stores it in our data property in milliseconds.

For this example, our HTML is once again pretty simple, as shown here:

```
<input type="text" ng-model="timeOfDay" time-picker />
```

Obviously, we'll also need to include the timepicker plugin within our main page so that it can be attached to our input, so if you're recreating the code on your own, be sure to do that before continuing on. For our directive, let's start with the basic definition object, and since we know we need data-binding functionality, we'll require ngModel from the start so that we can utilize its methods.

```
.directive('timePicker', function () {
  var today = new Date(new Date().toDateString());
  return {
    require : '?ngModel',
    link : function ($scope, $element, $attrs, ngModel) {
    }
  }
});
```

Note that since we need to be working with the actual instance of the element, almost all our code is going to sit inside the linking function, and we don't need to worry about the compilation process at all. We've also initialized a today variable that holds a Date object set to this morning at midnight. Creating the variable as part of the factory function allows us to just have one today variable that's shared across all instances of our time-picker directive. Be careful, however, as even though this allows us to minimize memory usage, it does mean that if our app is left open overnight, our directive will start providing inaccurate results. If you're planning on using this directive in a live application you'll want to create a secondary function that updates this value once tomorrow comes. Let's move forward now and grab our controller:

```
link : function ($scope, $element, $attrs, ngModel) {
  ngModel = ngModel || {
    "$setViewValue" : angular.noop
  }
}
```

You may have noticed this pattern before, as a part of the form and ngModel controllers that we looked at previously. Remember that we've made our controller requirement optional, so that if someone wants to use our directive just to attach a timepicker, but doesn't need the data-binding offered by ngModel, our directive won't throw an error when it doesn't find the requested controller. We could just use conditional statements to verify that ngModel is defined each time we need to use it, however the developers at Angular use this pattern, and I recommend it, in order to help keep the directive code a little cleaner. All we're doing here is saying that if ngModel is defined and has a true value, use that. If not, define it as an object with all of the requisite method names set to a no-op function (angular. noop is a convenience method provided for exactly this purpose). Now when we call ngModel.$setViewValue later in our directive, if there's no ngModel directive attached to our node, our code will continue along without an issue.

Speaking of ngModel.$setViewValue, let's take a look at how we'll attach our timepicker and where we might need that very function. If you've been pining away for a jQuery plugin while reading this book, now is the time for a brief moment of relief:

```
link : function ($scope, $element, $attrs, ngModel) {
  ...
  var initialized = false;
  setTimeout(function () {
    initialized = $element.timepicker()
      .on('changeTime', function (ev, ui) {
        var sec = $element.timepicker('getSecondsFromMidnight')
        ngModel.$setViewValue(sec * 1000);
      });
  });
}
```

Undoubtedly, your first question is going to be about setTimeout, particularly one with no actual timeout. Because we're in the linking function, our $element is fully instantiated, so this sort of trickery shouldn't be necessary. And you're right, it isn't necessary. It is, however, a practice I recommend, for two primary reasons. First, on occasion, particularly if your directive or another on your element is applying a template, Angular and jQuery will both try to apply themselves at the same time and you run into a race condition. While this is rare, and usually means that your plugin isn't actually working on the $element itself, but trying to clone it or nest something inside, it still can cause a few headaches and this helps guard against that.

Secondly, and more importantly, is that when you begin to develop larger applications and have hundreds or even thousands of different directive instances all manipulating and binding to their own elements in various ways, any plugin that requires DOM manipulation tends to slow things down. And often, especially for input type plugins that are hidden until the user directly interacts with them, these plugins can wait a few milliseconds to initialize themselves without harming the user experience. Wrapping our initialization process within `setTimeout` tells the JavaScript interpreter to process this after it's done with the current task, so the compilation process doesn't get delayed by our jQuery plugin attachment. Again, this isn't a necessity, but it is a practice I recommend you consider as you begin to develop larger applications with Angular.

Now that we've discussed that, let's take a look at how we're using `$setViewValue`. Because we've grabbed a shared instance of our `ngModel` controller, we can call the controller's `$setViewValue` function from our own directive, which helps us connect our plugin to the data model. Remember that this is used to take the display value, perform any necessary parsing, and then store it in the data property. The timepicker plugin emits a `changeTime` event anytime the user updates the time value displayed in our input, so we use that to know when we need to change our internal value. Within our event handler, all we have to do is get the number of seconds since midnight, which the plugin provides a convenience method for, then multiply it by a thousand and pass that into `$setViewValue`. Once we're done, our data will travel through the following process:

Once we have our timepicker initialized and listening for changes in the view, our next step is to define the `$render` method, which is responsible for converting a data value to the appropriate display or view value. This will be called any time the data value changes from a source outside our directive, including when it's first initialized and can be defined as follows:

```
link : function ($scope, $element, $attrs, ngModel) {
  ...
  ngModel.$render = function (val) {
    if (!initialized) {
```

```
    //If $render gets called before our timepicker plugin is ready,
just return
      return;
    };
    $element.timepicker('setTime', new Date(today.getTime() + val));
  }
}
```

Again, note that we're actually redefining the $render method of our shared ngModelController function, so when the ngModel directive observes a data change and tells the controller to execute $render, it's our function that gets called. All we have to do is know how to transform the data-model value into a value our plugin expects. In this case, the timepicker plugin provides a method for setting the time displayed by passing in a Date object with the specified time. Because our values are stored in milliseconds since midnight, when we need to render a value, we simply take the time from today, add on our new value, and create a Date object with that value. Again, when we're finished, our data will flow back into the view via the following process:

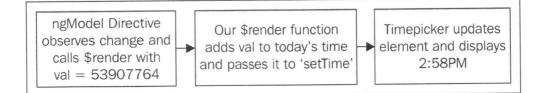

Summary

As you have hopefully seen, controllers provide a powerful mechanism for connecting two or more otherwise disconnected directives. This means that each directive can provide its own functionality, such as the simple timepicker plugin, but also extend its functionality if another directive is present. This targeted communication helps us make calls and interact with other pieces of an application directly without the need for the general broadcast approach provided by messaging. For the next chapter, we are moving on to a different topic entirely, transclusion, which allows you to utilize the existing content of an element when applying your directive.

7
Transclusion

Up to this point, we've primarily focused on one side of directives, which is how they can affect the elements to which they are attached by replacing the HTML via a template, binding additional plugins, or some combination of the two. In this chapter, we're going to look at the opposite side and see how transclusion allows for the original element's content to impact the behavior of the directive. While this methodology is certainly less common, it still is a powerful tool to be aware of and one you should call to mind when you find yourself tempted to create multiple directives that only vary from one another in content. With that, let's dive in and check out some examples.

That's not a word...

True. Looking up *transclude* in the dictionary won't help you understand what's really happening here (a fact lamented in the comment section on Angular's documentation site). I believe, however, that a brief dive into why they created this word in the first place will actually help greatly in your understanding of what its real purpose is, so bear with me a moment while we step aside from the focused realm of JavaScript and breathe deeply in the wider world of computer science.

If you've ever had the privilege, or arduous task, of creating a templating syntax, along with the parser required to bring that syntax to life, you're likely familiar with the concept of inclusion. Within a template, various snippets of code will often be repeated. In HTML, this is commonly seen with headers, footers, a Twitter widget, and so forth. And in the continuous quest for *Don't-Repeat-Yourself* code, we usually build 'include' commands into our templating definitions that allow you to write your snippet of code once and then drop it into other parts of your template wherever you want.

That part of templating, pretty much everyone agrees upon. There remains a question, however, which is: if you're including a snippet that itself has dynamic variables and needs to be parsed, what scope do you use when parsing it? Some widgets, such as the Twitter widget mentioned in the preceding paragraph, benefit from being parsed all by themselves in an isolated scope, and then just having the compiled result inserted at the include tag. Other widgets, such as a customized blog post header or dynamic list display, however, need to be parsed within the original scope of the include tag, not outside of it. Most mature templating syntaxes have ways of performing both types of inclusion, but it's a problem that each syntax designer must answer in their own way.

...it is a solution

For Angular that answer is transclusion. My unofficial interpretation of the word is *translated-inclusion*. What transclusion does is offer a way to create a widget with an isolate scope, which we as good modular developers always do, but then tunnel back out into the parent scope to parse the original content. This, of course, is significantly clearer in an example, so let's check one out. Take a look at the following HTML and note what's different from our previous examples:

```
<div>
  <input type="text" ng-model="name" />
  <select ng-model="movie">
    <option value="Man Of Steel">Superman</option>
    <option value="A New Hope">Star Wars</option>
  </select>
  <input type="number" ng-model="friendCount" />
</div>
<div movie-info="movie">
  <p>Hi, I'm {{name}}, and I'm going to see {{movie}} with
{{friendCount}} friends</p>
</div>
```

Ok, so what do you notice? Hopefully, one of the main things you saw is that our directive, `movie-info`, isn't just an empty node this time. It has child nodes. Before we get too much farther into how exactly that impacts our development, however, let's take a look at the directive definition as well:

```
directive('movieInfo', function () {
  return {
    template : '<div class="movie-info">' +
      '<h1 class="movie-title">{{name}}</h1>' +
      '<img class="movie-poster" ng-src="posters/{{name}}.jpg" />' +
      '<div ng-transclude></div>' +
    '</div>',
```

```
    transclude : true,
    scope : {
      'name' : '=movieInfo'
    }
  }
});
```

Now I should ask again, what do you notice? Perhaps most notably, we have a scoping issue. On the one hand, we're adhering to our principle of modularity and isolating our scope. On the other hand, however, we've ignorantly introduced a naming conflict. Both scopes use the `name` property, and even though our scope is isolated, the origin element content we've pulled in is now inside our directive element, so surely it's going to be parsed against the directive scope, which isn't the `name` property we want.

Enter transclusion, stage left. Remember, we said that transclusion stands for translated-inclusion, which means that first we parse it and then we include it. In the official Angular documentation, they explain this by saying that the transcluded scope and the isolate scope are siblings. The transcluded scope inherits from the parent scope per normal, and the isolate scope, though still a child of the parent scope, is otherwise disconnected.

That undoubtedly sounds fascinating, but perhaps a bit obtuse. Let's take a look then, at what our HTML will look like after everything is parsed and compiled, taking note of the highlighted values:

```
<div>
  <input type="text" ng-model="name" /><!-- value: "Alex" -->
  <select ng-model="movie">
    <option value="Superman">Man of Steel</option><!-- selected -->
    <option value="Star Wars">A New Hope</option>
  </select>
  <input type="number" ng-model="friendCount" /><!-- value: 3 -->
</div>
<div movie-info="movie">
    <div class="movie-info">
        <!-- these two lines parse against the directive scope -->
        <h1 class="movie-title">Superman</h1>
        <img class="movie-poster" src="posters/Superman.jpg" />
        <div ng-transclude>
          <!-- Everything in here parses against the parent scope -->
          <p>Hi, I'm Alex, and I'm going to see Superman with 3
friends</p>
        </div>
    </div>
</div>
```

As this hopefully makes clearer, we've effectively created a tunnel to the parent scope, hidden from the directive's scope and yet fully accessible to the transcluded portion nested inside. And, of course, all these data values are dynamic, so if the user selects a different movie, all the instances of Superman will change to Star Wars, whether they're bound to the movie property of the parent scope or the name property of the directive scope. Likewise, changing the parent scope's name property will only affect the value within our transcluded element, the directive scope will remain ignorant of its existence entirely.

Manipulating the transcluded content

Sometimes you want more control over the transcluded content than just dropping it into an element and calling it a day. There are a couple of different methods you can use, but I've found the most efficient and straightforward is by utilizing the directive controller. As you likely remember from the previous chapter, one of the main benefits of controllers is that they can be shared across directives. Another feature, not as commonly used, is that they can also require $transclude, which provides a transclusion function already properly bound to the parent scope and ready for use.

Again, you'll really only need to utilize this functionality when you want to manipulate the transcluded content before including it in your new directive element, otherwise the standard procedure we used in the preceding section is far simpler and easier to debug. That said, let's take a look at a situation where this can come in handy. Consider that you have a blog header that you want to enhance. Your starting HTML might look like the following:

```
<div class="post">
  <h2 class="post-header">
    <span class="title">{{postTitle}}</span> |
    <span class="author">{{author}}</span>
    <span class="date">{{formattedDate}}</span>
  </h2>
  <div class="content">...</div>
</div>
```

While that conveys all the necessary information, it's rather boring. Suppose you want to only show the title normally, then when your devoted reader scrolls down to a specific post, the title slides to the center and your author and date values fade in on the sides (If you're a designer, apologies for my admittedly developer-brained invention here). While you could try using a series of regular jQuery plugins for this, hopefully by this point in our book you've become so awed by the structure that Angular provides for modularity that your days of non-data-driven plugin-binding are a thing of the past. If not, humor me for the sake of our example.

So, you want this awesome blog post header and you've got the plugins ready for detecting scroll positions and fading in your metadata; the only trick is that they all work much better together if your HTML actually looks like this:

```
<div class="post">
  <div class="post-header">
    <span class="date" style="display:none;">{{formattedDate}}</span>
    <h2 class="title">{{postTitle}}</h2>
    <span class="author" style="display:none;">{{author}}</span>
  </div>
  <div class="content">...</div>
</div>
```

With the power of controller fueled transclusion, we can do just that. Remember, when we request $transclude, it's already bound correctly, so even if we have other directive scope properties in here, they won't conflict with our post values. And for those of you craving a bit of jQuery based DOM manipulation, this next slice of example code is my gift to you:

```
.directive('postHeader', function () {
  var tpl = '<div class="post-header"></div>';
  return {
    template : tpl,
    replace : true,
    restrict : 'C',//We're attaching ourselves to the classname 'post-
header' here
    transclude : 'element',//We want the whole element, not just the
content
    controller : function ($scope, $element, $attrs, $transclude) {
      $transclude(function (clone) {
        //clone is our transcluded element, in this case the h2 tag,
fully compiled and ready for use
        clone.removeClass('post-header');// this class is on our main
directive element now
        var title = clone.find('.title').text();
        var dateEl = clone.find('.date').hide();//Start hidden
        var authorEl = clone.find('.author').hide();
        // Now insert them all in where we want them
        $element
          .append(dateEl)
          .append('<h2 class="title">'+title + '</h2>')
          .append(authorEl);
      });
      //When a user scrolls down to our element, reveal author and
date
```

```
$element.waypoint(function () {
  $element.find('.date, .author').fadeIn();
});
    }
  }
});
```

Summary

As you can see, once we've grabbed $transclude, the rest of the manipulations are actually quite standard. In this case, because we've distributed the transcluded content in a piecemeal manner, we end up not even ever inserting the clone element itself back into the DOM; however there might be other times when you only want to extract part of the element for use elsewhere, and then insert the rest back into its normal location. In either case, always remember that transclusion is your friend when you need to interact with the content internal to your directive. Use the standard ng-transclude directive when you want the content unaltered, and controller plus $transclude if you need to manipulate it first. Coming up next we're going to spend two chapters talking about testing, both unit testing and Angular's scenario end-to-end testing framework.

8
Good Karma – Testing in AngularJS

Ah, testing! The process that every young developer believes they don't need; of course, every experienced developer just looks at them and says, "Just wait, you'll see." Often, however, experienced or not, testing is one of the last tasks we as developers think about, if for no other reason than because it tends to feel like a whole new development task, and even worse, one where perhaps your client or boss thinks you're wasting time because they can't see the direct results. In an effort to help assuage this suffering, Angular comes shipped with Karma, a test runner built to make testing easier and designed to make testing as easy as just scoping out the desired functionality, and instead of being a part of the process that drags down your morale, it gives you immediate feedback on the effectiveness, or not-quite-there-yet-ness, of your code, which quickly makes for faster and more efficient development overall.

Getting Started

Now that we have the obligatory testing-is-good platitudes out the way, let's dive into **Karma** and let it prove its worth on its own. If you already have **NPM (Node Package Manager)** installed, installing Karma is as simple as `npm install -g karma`. If not, head over to `http://karma-runner.github.io` and follow the instructions there. Once you have it installed, fire up a terminal in the same directory as your code and run `karma start`, then sit back and watch the magic happen.

Well, sort of. Likely what really happened was you got an error saying it couldn't find your config file. Karma is designed to let you specify different configurations for each project. Many of the options are more niche than we're going to cover in this chapter, but let's walk through some of the basic options that need to be defined for every project.

Configuration

By default, Karma looks for a configuration file called `karma.conf.js`, and while you can name it whatever you want, we're going to stick with that for the sake of convenience. To create your initial file, run `karma init` in your project directory and answer the questions appropriately. For this chapter, I'll be using the following configuration:

- Testing framework: `Jasmine`
- Use Require.js: `no`
- Browser: `Chrome`
- Files to test: `test/spec/**/*.js`
- Watch files and run on change: `yes`

These are the defaults for my current version of Karma, though they may change by the time you're reading this. When you specify which file pattern to watch, it will likely create a warning that it can't find any files that match that pattern. That's ok, we'll get to that in a moment. First, we need to create our code directory, import Angular, and finally tell Karma to grab our libraries so it can process our code correctly.

Angular and Karma

First, go ahead and create a directory called `app`, where we'll store all our application code. Within that, let's create a `components` directory for Angular (and jQuery if you need it) and a `scripts` directory for all our custom code. Go ahead and import your `angular.js` file, as well as the `angular-mocks` file included in your Angular download (if you just downloaded the base `angular.js` file, you'll need to go back to `http://www.angularjs.org` and download the entire ZIP package).

 Some of you may recognize this filesystem pattern as the one followed by **Bower** (`http://bower.io`), an awesome browser package manager by Twitter. We don't have time here to dive into it deeper, but I highly recommend you look into it as you go forward in developing your web applications.

Once you have everything included, your directory structure should look something like the following:

```
myAwesomeApp/
-- test/
```

```
---- spec/
------ directives/
-------- directives.js (currently an empty file)
-- app/
---- components/
------ angular/
-------- angular.js
------ angular-mocks/
-------- angular-mocks.js
---- scripts/
------ app.js (currently an empty file)
------ directives/
-------- directives.js
```

I've gone ahead and created a couple of empty test and app files as well. You're welcome to organize your app and test directories however you want, although I do recommend keeping them in a similar structure to help you remember which files test which parts of your application.

Now that our directory structure is in place, we need to finish telling Karma which files to include. Go ahead and open karma.conf.js again in a text editor and find the files array. Right now it should just have one entry, corresponding to the test file pattern we specified in the previous paragraph. Now, before that entry, let's add the file patterns for our application scripts, so it should read like this:

```
files = [
  'app/components/angular/angular.js',
  'app/components/angular-mocks/angular-mocks.js',
  'app/scripts/*.js',
  'app/scripts/**/*.js',
  'test/spec/**/*.js'
];
```

And, just like that, Karma is ready to run. That said, a test setup without any tests is obviously not particularly helpful, so let's go ahead and create our first test.

 If the idea of writing a test before you've even written any application code seems backwards to you, I highly recommend doing some research into **Test Driven Development (TDD)** online. We don't have time to cover it all here, but it is the approach we'll use for these two chapters and our final app in the last chapter.

My first test

There are two primary types of tests supported by Angular and Karma: Unit and E2E (end-to-end). Unit testing is concerned with testing small chunks of code to ensure they do, and continue to do, what they're supposed to do. We'll do a quick overview of those next, and then dive into them in more detail in the next chapter. After our unit testing overview, we're going to introduce Angular's approach to E2E testing, which ensures that your whole application has and maintains all its functionality. Because E2E testing is more focused on an entire application, and not just a single directive, we won't spend too much time with it here, but it is worth being familiar with as you go forward.

Ok, let's take a look at some code. Jasmine allows you to have multiple test blocks, each of which is housed in a `describe` call. Usually you would use one test block per module of code, unless you have some modules of either very large or very small size. For our purposes, we'll wrap all our directive tests in one `describe` call, so that our initial `test/spec/directives/directives.js` file looks like the following:

```
describe('My Tested Directive', function () {
});
```

Since we're going to be testing a directive, we'll need access to the compilation process, as well as a scope to work with. Luckily for us, the `angular-mocks` package we included provides the same dependency injection functionality that we've come to appreciate so much in our application code, using the `inject` method as highlighted in the following code snippet:

```
describe('My Tested Directive', function () {
  var $compile, $rootScope;

  //Require the module our directive is attached to
  beforeEach(module('myApp'));

  //The inject function strips away the underscores, which allows us
  //to avoid any scoping confusion
  beforeEach(inject(function (_$compile_, _$rootScope_) {
      $compile = _$compile_;
      $rootScope = _$rootScope_;
    }));
});
```

The module method is also provided by the angular-mocks package, and bootstraps our Angular app for us before running each of the tests. The mocks package provides a few other utilities for testing which we won't cover here, but are helpful if you dive into more complex testing situations and are documented as part of the official Angular documentation. Finally, the beforeEach method is part of the Jasmine framework itself and, as you might guess by the name, executes before each test runs, allowing us to perform any necessary setup or data normalization before continuing.

Now that we have everything wired up, let's go ahead and write our first unit test. For this directive, we're going create another listing directive, much like out tweet widget from *Chapter 2, The Need for Directives*, except this time it's a list of players, and we'll build the entire widget as a tested directive, instead of just generic Angular code. Our first test simply confirms that our directive compiled correctly.

```
describe('My Tested Directive', function () {
  ... //setup code

  //We'll use this template for all our tests
  var directiveTpl = '<div player-widget="playerList"></div>';
  it('should create player widget element', function () {
    var $scope = $rootScope.$new();
    //The passing a template into $compile returns a "linking"
function that can
    //be used to take a scope and apply it to the template
    var $element = $compile(directiveTpl)($scope);
    //Now the actual test
    expect($element.html()).toContain('class="player-widget"');
  });
});
```

Now, if Karma is running in the background, you'll see it noticed the new test, ran it, and found the result a bit disappointing. That, of course, is exactly what we expected, since we haven't defined our directive or its actual template yet. In order to prevent our dear test runner from being sad for too long, let's go ahead and build that out. In our scripts/app.js file, we need to create a module named myApp, and then in the scripts/directives/directives.js file, we'll create our actual directive. As an exercise to test your progress on the path to directive mastery, go ahead and build part of the directive yourself so that our tests start passing. If you get stuck, don't worry, we'll walk through all the code shortly, but first, try it yourself, and then we'll write a few more tests.

Mocking data

Often when we're testing different pieces of an application, we need to validate how that piece responds to specific data input. We don't however, want to be dependent on an external source for that data; there's nothing worse than spending several hours trying to debug your failing tests only to realize that your third-party data is corrupt. Because of this, whenever possible we want to use mocked sample data for our tests so that we can be sure of the validity, or invalidity if we're negative testing, of the input our directive is receiving.

> As a side note, whenever possible your directive should not be responsible for actually retrieving the information. Angular provides services as a more modular way of handling information, and they also make it significantly easier to test. We don't have time for a full discussion of services here, but the short answer is if you find yourself requiring $http into your directive, it's time to create a service.

In our case here, we'll want to mock the player JSON data that gets passed into our widget. For convenience' sake, we'll include our sample data in the same file as our test, but if you have lots of sample data I recommend keeping it in separate files and loading it into your test runner via the karma.conf.js config as discussed previously.

For our next two tests then, we want to ensure that our directive properly received the player list, and that it correctly generated the corresponding DOM elements.

```
describe('My Tested Directive', function () {
  … //setup work and first test

  var playerList;
  beforeEach(function () {
    //We want to set this before each test, in case we need to
manipulate it
    playerList = [
      { "name" : "Babe Ruth", "team" : "Yankees" },
      { "name" : "Jackie Robinson", "team" : "Dodgers" },
      { "name" : "Hank Aaron", "team" : "Braves" }
    ];
  });
  it('should scope playerList to players', function () {
    var $parent = $rootScope.$new();
```

```
    $parent.playerList = playerList;
    var $element = $compile(directiveTpl)($parent);
    var $directiveScope = $element.scope(); //Angular provides the
scope() method to retrieve an element's scope
    expect($directiveScope.players).toBeDefined();//Confirm we have a
new property
    expect($directiveScope.players.length).toEqual(playerList.
length);//Confirm our list is the same length
  });
  it('should generate player elements for each player', function () {
    var $scope = $rootScope.$new();
    $scope.playerList = playerList;
    var $element = $compile(directiveTpl)($scope);
    //We're outside of the angular $watch loop here, so we need to
call $digest manually
    $scope.$digest();
    //the jQLite wrapper provided by angular can only find elements by
tag name. If you're including jQuery, you'll have access to those full
methods instead
    var $players = $element.find('p');
    expect($players.length).toEqual(playerList.length);
    expect($players.eq(0).text()).toContain('Babe Ruth');
  });
});
```

Before we go on, a quick note about testing objects and using equality. Jasmine is good about using an object's properties, not its reference, to test for equality. That said, the ng-repeat directive adds an extra $$hashKey property to each item for caching purposes, so if you're going to test a property that you iterate over (like we do here), it likely won't be the same as what was passed in, which is why we used definition and length tests, instead of just expect($directiveScope.players).toEqual($parent.playerList).

The test subject

Ok, so we've once again caused our poor test runner extensive grief and anguish (we now have two failing tests, not just the paltry one from earlier), so let's dive into our directive code and see how this all fits together. As a confirmation to what you've hopefully already coded, the scripts/app.js file should be one simple line:

```
angular.module('myApp', []);
```

And then our final `scripts/directives/directives.js` file should have come together somewhat similar to the following:

```
angular.module('myApp')
  .directive('playerWidget', function () {
    //Define our template for the widget
    var tpl = '<div class="player-widget">' +
      '<p class="player" ng-repeat="p in players">' +
        '{{p.name}} ({{p.team}})' +
      '</p>' +
    '</div>';
    return {
      template : tpl,
      scope : {
        'players' : '=playerWidget'//Declare our two-way binding, and
nothing else
      }
    }
  });
```

With that, we're going to press pause on our study of unit testing. We'll dive back in more deeply in the next chapter, but first, I want to introduce the Angular Scenario test runner, and its usage for E2E testing.

E2E testing

For E2E testing, Angular provides a testing suite called the **Scenario Runner**, which is essentially a collection of utilities to navigate your application and interact with it programmatically, so that you can test functionality from the user's point of view as well, and not just at the code level.

To get the Scenario Runner configured, go ahead and copy your current `karma.conf.js` to `karma-e2e.conf.js`. This testing setup requires a few different files to operate, and it's generally recommended to keep your two configurations separate for modularity and ease of testing. Open your new configuration file and replace `jasmine` with `ng-scenario` in the `frameworks` array. You can also remove all the application files from the include, as we're going to be loading our app directly this time, so those includes are all handled via the application itself. Now is a good time to also create an `e2e` directory under your `test` folder and update the test path to match it. Our files array should now have only one element:

```
files = [
  'test/e2e/**/*.js'
];
```

Now, there's one last thing we need to do to get this all running, and that's make sure our app is hosted somewhere that a browser can access. To do this, set up a proxy between what Karma sees as your application root and the actual web address (including port) for your application. The following two examples are for Apache and `node.js` servers. If you get stuck, a quick Google search for your specific setup should point you in the right direction.

//Included in your `karma-e2e.conf.js` file (only use one of the two below)

```
proxies : {
  '/': 'http://localhost/my-app/' // For apache/nginx
  '/': 'http://localhost:8080/' // For node.js
}
```

Now that Karma is all set for our E2E testing extravaganza, let's give it something to work with.

 If you get an error when running this configuration that says
`No provider for "framework:ng-scenario"`, execute
`npm install karma-ng-scenario karma-ng-html2js-preprocessor` in your application directory, and then run `karma start karma-e2e.conf.js` again.

Scenarios

We'll start by testing the same functionality we covered in the previous section, except now from the browser's point-of-view. We'll need to have an actual `index.html` file which contains our widget, so go ahead and create that now if you're following along (and you are, of course, aren't you?). Then let's create our first few tests as follows:

```
describe('My Tested Widget', function () {
  beforeEach(function () {
    browser().navigateTo('../../app/index.html');
  }); // Tell our testing browser to load the index file

  it('Should display the widget', function () {
    expect(element('.player-widget').count()).toBe(1);
  });

  it('Should display 3 players', function () {
    expect(repeater('.player-widget .player').count()).toBe(3);
  });
});
```

So far everything looks pretty much the same as our previous unit tests, except that now everything is already compiled and we don't have to worry about generating all our elements. Another gotcha to be aware of is that while these tests look just like Jasmine, they have one key difference: `expect` here requires a future, not a value. What this means is that the usually tautological test of `expect(true).toBe(true)` will actually fail, because the first `true` is a value. Instead, the Scenario Runner version of `expect` requires a future, or promise, which will eventually resolve to a value and it's that resolved value that gets tested against the expectation. If you're not familiar with promises, I recommend taking some time to learn about them, as both Angular and jQuery (and several other JavaScript libraries) use them for nearly all asynchronous processing.The Scenario Runner uses them because it actually queues up all the tests, and then runs through them, instead of just processing them as it reads them, so the values need to be resolved asynchronously. All the standard Scenario Runner methods return futures, so usually you won't need to worry about it, but it is something to be aware of as you start developing more complex tests.

Finally, let's add one more test, looking at actual user interaction. Suppose we want to highlight a player when the user clicks on it. As you can see in the following code snippet, the Scenario Runner provides many of the same methods you might have used in jQuery DOM manipulation, such as `click` and `attr`:

```
...
it('Should highlight a player when clicked', function () {
  var p = element('.player-widget .player:first');
  p.click() ;
  expect(p.attr('class')).toContain('highlighted') ;
});
...
```

Just like that, we've loaded our page, interacted with it, and tested the result. I'll leave it to you to update our widget directive with the code to satisfy Karma's need for properly executing code.

Summary

So now we've introduced Karma, gone over its basic configuration options, and looked at the basics for both unit and E2E testing. While unit testing allows us to validate the data-model, E2E testing lets us test what the user actually sees, in a way that's fast and reliable. Next, we'll dive into unit testing in more detail, looking at how we can use it to ensure both accurate and corrupt data is handled cleanly by our directives.

9
A Deeper Dive into Unit Testing

In the previous chapter we discussed the basics of testing with Angular, including how to set up Karma and write your first few unit and E2E tests. For the next few pages we're going to dive deeper into the realm of unit testing, taking a look at some of the ways being data-driven makes our lives easier, and how striving to make our code easy to test will also directly lead to our code also being more modular and extensible. We'll continue using Jasmine for all our tests here, and many of the examples we cover will be helpful for testing in all frameworks, not just Angular, although of course that will be our primary focus.

Highlighted, again

At the end of our discussion on E2E testing, we added the ability to highlight each player when a user clicked on it. I left it up to you to implement the directive code to create that functionality, and hopefully by now you've done so. There are a couple ways you might have gone about it and, if you're used to the DOM manipulation method of user-interaction, you might have written something like the following:

```
directive('playerWidget', function () {
  var tpl = '<div class="player-widget">' +
    '<p class="player" ng-repeat="p in players">' +
      '{{p.name}} ({{p.team}})' +
    '</p>' +
  '</div>';
  return {
    template : tpl,
    scope : {
```

```
    'players' : '=playerWidget',
  },
  link : function ($scope, $element, $attrs) {
    //When a user clicks the player tag, add the highlighted class
    $element.on('click','.player', function (ev) {
      jQuery(ev.currentTarget).addClass('highlighted');
    });


  }

  }
});
```

And while that method will work, and even passes our E2E tests, nothing in the data-model itself actually changes to correspond to the highlighted state, which makes it virtually impossible to test from a strictly data-model perspective, making unit testing worthless for this functionality.

What Angular encourages, both from a modularity perspective and for ease of testing, is a more data-driven approach. Consider the following example instead, with the changed portions highlighted:

```
directive('playerWidget', function () {
  var tpl = '<div class="player-widget">' +
      '<p class="player" ng-repeat="p in players" ng-
class="{highlighted : p.active}" ng-click="activate(p)">' +
        '{{p.name}} ({{p.team}})' +
      '</p>' +
    '</div>';
  return {
    template : tpl,
    scope : {
      'players' : '=playerWidget',
    },
    link : function ($scope, $element, $attrs) {
      //When a user clicks, set the active flag on the player object
      $scope.activate = function (player) {
        player.active = true;
      }
    }
  }
});
```

Now we can write a simple test to validate our activate method as follows:

```
it('should activate the player', function () {
    var $scope = $rootScope.$new();
    $scope.playerList = playerList;
    var $element = $compile(directiveTpl)($scope);
    var $directiveScope = $element.scope();
    var firstPlayer = $directiveScope.players[0];
    //First validate that the active property is either false or
undefined
    expect(firstPlayer.active).toBeFalsy();
    $directiveScope.activate(firstPlayer);
    //Now confirm that we've set that same property to true
    expect(firstPlayer.active).toBe(true);
});
```

This approach to development and testing allows us to use unit tests to confirm that our data-model is accurate and properly manipulated, and then use E2E tests to validate the end result. As your applications get more complex, when something breaks an E2E test, you'll want unit tests like these to help highlight exactly where the problem is, instead of having to walk through a long function chain step-by-step.

Negative testing

Generally, when we first start testing, we think of all the things that need to happen and then test for them, which is an awesome start. What we often forget however, is that we need to decide, and test for, what happens when something goes wrong, or when that 'it-could-never-happen' case happens. Consider our player list and what would happen if we received a player object without a team. There are plenty of reasons why this might happen—they're undrafted, a database corruption, or your data-entry intern missed their coffee that morning—but, whatever the reason, we need to make sure our directive can handle it cleanly. Right now, if we were to pass that in, we'd end up with the following rather unprofessional output:

```
...
<p class="player">John Smith ()</p>
...
```

Since we'd rather not have a bunch of empty parentheses floating around in our application, let's update our directive and tests to only display the team name, and wrapping parentheses, when there's actually a team value associated with that player.

First, let's write our test and see what that tells us.

```
...
var playerList;
beforeEach(function () {
  //We've updated this to include a fourth player without a team
  playerList = [
    { "name" : "Babe Ruth", "team" : "Yankees" },
    { "name" : "Jackie Robinson", "team" : "Dodgers" },
    { "name" : "Hank Aaron", "team" : "Braves" },
    { "name" : "John Smith"}
  ];
});
...
it('should display team when present', function () {
  var $scope = $rootScope.$new();
  $scope.playerList = playerList;
  var $element = $compile(directiveTpl)($scope);
  $scope.$digest();
  var $players = $element.find('p');
  expect($players.eq(0).text()).toContain(playerList[0].team);
});

it('should not display team when not present', function () {
  var $scope = $rootScope.$new();
  $scope.playerList = playerList;
  var $element = $compile(directiveTpl)($scope);
  $scope.$digest();
  var $players = $element.find('p');
  expect($players.eq(3).text()).not.toContain('()');
});
```

Naturally, if we run this right now, it will fail. More importantly, however, it also feels very fragile. Testing for the existence of ' () ' makes us very dependent on the specific styling implementation, and means that a layout change could easily *break* our tests without actually breaking any of the real functionality in our code. With that in mind, let's try to update our directive template a bit and see if we can make it, and our test, more flexible.

The main problem we have in the preceding example is that our team description is just hanging out there all by itself, so a simple fix would be to wrap it in a DOM element that we can easily query for.

```
...
var tpl = '<div class="player-widget">' +
  '<p class="player" ng-repeat="p in players" ng-click="activate(p)"
ng-class="{highlighted : p.active}">' +
    '{{p.name}} <span class="team" ng-show="p.team">({{p.team}})</
span>' +
  '</p>' +
'</div>';
...
```

Wrapping our team name up in its own element allows us to create much cleaner and more flexible tests, which won't break the moment we need to change our parentheses to brackets or remove them altogether.

```
it('should display team when present', function () {
  var $scope = $rootScope.$new();
  $scope.playerList = playerList;
  var $element = $compile(directiveTpl)($scope);
  $scope.$digest();
  var $players = $element.find('p');
  var teamNode = $players.eq(0).find('span');
  expect(teamNode.text()).toContain(playerList[0].team);
});

it('should not display team when not present', function () {
  var $scope = $rootScope.$new();
  $scope.playerList = playerList;
  var $element = $compile(directiveTpl)($scope);
  $scope.$digest();
  var $players = $element.find('p');
  var teamNode = $players.eq(3).find('span');
  expect(teamNode.css('display')).toBe('none');
});
```

Summary

Obviously, these few pages are far too short to dive very far into the complexities of unit testing; hopefully, however, this has given you a taste of the various approaches you can take and reinforced for you why our original principle of data-driven modularity is so important. As a final note on testing, because we're using Jasmine for all our unit tests, all of Jasmine's functionality is still available, including custom matchers and spies. In the next chapter, we're going to wrap-up our study on directives by building a full featured module from scratch, making use of everything we've learned so far, and discovering a few new awesome tricks along the way as well.

10
Bringing it All Together

Congratulations. You've made it nearly the entire way through our study of Angular Directives. No doubt some parts are still somewhat confusing, and there are likely other areas you're already tired of hearing about (did I mention that you should practice data-driven modularity?), but despite all that, hopefully you've come this far excited about the possibilities in front of you. Whether you intend to spend the rest of your days with Angular or just wanted to gain a different perspective that you can take back to the framework in your life, hopefully this book has been an aid in that process so far. What I want to do for this chapter now is to walk through the entire directive creation process, from our first tests all the way through to a complete module. I highly encourage you to follow along with your own development tools of choice, but if you get stuck or want to come back and review something, all of the code created in this chapter is available at `https://github.com/mrvdot/angular-content-grid/`. We'll be working through an actual Angular module that's live on **GitHub**, so the final code here will likely be different from what you see online. To help you see each step as we progress, I've created tags within the repository that you can use to track our progress throughout this chapter. If you want to be able to follow along with each step, go ahead and run the following code in your working directory before moving on:

```
# git clone https://github.com/mrvdot/angular-content-grid/
....
# cd angular-content-grid
# git checkout blankRepo
```

The last command will update your working directory to the `blankRepo` tag, which represents the initial commit with nothing more than a `README` file.

 If you don't use `git`, or have simply downloaded the code packet for this book already, all the branches have been included in the `C10` directory within that packet as well.

Angular content grid

For this chapter then, we're going to build a content grid, utilizing the awesome jQuery Masonry plugin by David DeSandro. At the end, we want the ability to pass in a dynamic array of HTML elements, display them, trigger Masonry to organize them properly, and communicate with the rest of our app that everything is processed and ready, allowing for custom hooks into the Masonry process. Once done, we should be able to render multiple elements on to a page like you see here:

Moby Dick	War of the Worlds pt 1	War of the Worlds pt 2
Though Stubb did not understand the BOUTON part of the inscription, yet the word ROSE, and the bulbous figure-head put together, sufficiently explained the whole to him.	I and my wife stood amazed. Then I realised that the crest of Maybury Hill must be within range of the Martians' Heat-Ray now that the college was cleared out of the way.	At that I gripped my wife's arm, and without ceremony ran her out into the road. Then I out the servant, telling her I would go upsta myself for the box she was clamouring for.
"A wooden rose-bud, eh?" he cried with his hand to his nose, "that will do very well; but how like all creation it smells!"	**War of the Worlds pt 3**	**More Moby Dick**
	"We can't possibly stay here," I said; and as I spoke the firing reopened for a moment upon the common.	Now in order to hold direct communication people on deck, he had to pull round the bo the starboard side, and thus come close to blasted whale; and so talk over it.

[04:53:11 PM] Masonry Initialized

[04:53:11 PM] Masonry Updated to include 5 elements

Diving in

With that, let's go ahead and dive into writing some code to build this... Wait, you know better than that. We just spent two chapters on the value of testing and the importance of writing those tests before our code; surely you haven't forgotten all that already. So instead, let's write up some unit tests to serve as our initial specification. If you're following along on your own machine, you'll need to setup Karma as before, or just copy our last setup over and rename the files. Once you have that ready and Karma running, let's create a unit test file with two initial tests:

```
describe('Content Grid', function () {
  var $compile
    , $rootScope
    , tpl = '<div content-grid="elements"></div>'
    , elements = [];

  beforeEach(module('mvdContentGrid'))
```

```
beforeEach(inject(function (_$compile_, _$rootScope_) {
  $compile = _$compile_;
  $rootScope = _$rootScope_;
}));

describe('Basic compilation', function () {
  it('should scope elements correctly', function () {
    var $parScope = $rootScope.$new();
    $parScope.elements = elements;
    $parScope.otherProperty = "should be undefined";
    var $el = $compile(tpl)($parScope);
    var $scope = $el.scope();
    expect($scope.elements.length).toBe($parScope.elements.length);
    $parScope.elements.push({"test" : "item"});
    expect($scope.elements.length).toBe($parScope.elements.length);
    expect($scope.otherProperty).toBeUndefined();
  });

  it('should compile template with elements', function () {
    var $parScope = $rootScope.$new();
    $parScope.elements = [
        {
          title : "TITLE",
          id : 1,
          content : "<p>CONTENT</p>"
        }
    ]
    var $el = $compile(tpl)($parScope);
    $rootScope.$digest();
    var gridElements = $el.find('[content-grid-element]');
    expect(gridElements.length).toBe($parScope.elements.length);
    var first = $parScope.elements[0];
    expect(gridElements.eq(0).data('element-id')).toBe(first.id);
    expect(gridElements.eq(0).find('.title').text()).toBe(first.
title);
    expect(gridElements.eq(0).find('.content').html()).
toContain(first.content);
  });
});
```

These two initial tests ensure a few basic things about our directive. First, that it will initialize and be properly scoped. We do this by testing for the existence and proper linkage of the `elements` property that we want to be passed through, as well as ensuring that other properties don't make it through to our directive's scope. Secondly, we use the second test to validate that our content grid will iterate through all the elements and create actual DOM grid elements containing their content. You may notice that we've used jQuery selectors instead of sticking with the standard jqLite selectors provided within Angular. This is because we'll use jQuery within the directive itself, and since its selectors are significantly more powerful, I find it makes the testing code much cleaner to use those instead.

You may also have noticed that at this point our tests do nothing to test for the Masonry functionality. There are two main reasons for this, and as you go forward with Angular directives you'll likely find these apply to almost any directive with a significant third-party plugin component integration:

1. First, we (or, at least, I) simply don't know how Masonry operates well enough yet to know how to test for it. This is often the case when integrating with plugins, and for this I find it easier and more efficient to simply set the integration tests aside until we've actually connected it (even if only through the browser development tools) and can better say how it's working on our element(s).

2. Secondly, we're just not ready yet. Our goal at this point is to create a working directive, and while the integration is a key piece of that, it's not the first step. My strategy for TDD is write one or two tests, then the code to satisfy those, and then go on. Some people have recommended writing out the entire specification in tests first, and while you're certainly welcome to experiment with that, I usually find that that can cause almost as much frustration as not testing at all.

The initial directive

Now that we have our first couple tests ready and running, let's move forward with the directive code. I won't include every line of the directive here, just the key pieces for the sake of space. To review all the code, run `git checkout initialTests` within your cloned repository directory. Now, without further ado, the directive is:

```
angular.module('mvdContentGrid', ['ngSanitize'])
  .directive('contentGrid', function () {
    return {
      template : /* ... */,
      replace : true,
      scope : {
        'elements' : '=contentGrid'
      }
    }
  })
  .directive('contentGridElement', function () {
    return {
      template : /* ... */,
      replace : true,
      scope : {
        'contentElement' : '=contentGridElement'
      },
      link : function ($scope, $element, $attrs) {
        $element.data('element-id', $scope.contentElement.id);
      }
    }
  });
```

There are a couple important things here to notice. First, we have required `ngSanitize` into our module, which provides us with the ability to bind filtered HTML to an element. Any time you're going to be binding HTML straight from a data source to your elements, I highly recommend you use the sanitize filter to ensure no malicious, or even just malformed, code gets in. To see how exactly we're using it within this directive, check out the template for the `content-grid-element` directive. Secondly, we're using two separate directives for additional modularity. This isn't always necessary but, in many cases I do recommend using this approach to help separate out responsibilities and keep your code cleaner. Finally, you may wonder why we used the `.data()` method on our element, when everything is supposed to be pulled directly from the data-model anyway. In short, it's because we often integrate with plugins/libraries that don't have easy access to the Angular scope, and for small data pieces such as an ID, making them easily retrievable to third-party plugins actually tends to help keep our code more modular, rather than less.

Connecting Masonry

At this point, we have a functioning directive that takes an array of content elements and displays them. That's great, but it's still missing the key piece: our Masonry integration. If you haven't already, go ahead and download the packaged JavaScript file from `http://masonry.desandro.com`. While Masonry can also be installed using Bower, it has several dependencies and requires a fuller build process, which is outside the scope of this book, so for now we'll just use the already packaged file.

Any time you want to connect a DOM manipulation plugin, there are a few things to keep in mind:

1. Identify both the initialization and update methods for your plugin. Sometimes these are the same.

2. Evaluate if the plugin needs to be told explicitly about changes, or if it will detect them itself.

3. Set up the appropriate watchers to initialize and update your plugin.

To do this, we'll use both the `controller` and `link` properties of our `content-grid` directive. The shared `controller` function allows us to manage all the options in a way that can be accessed by each of the element directives easily, as well as provide any connection methods we might need. We use `link`, however, because we know it won't be called until our element is fully compiled and inserted into the DOM, so we can safely call our initialization methods there. At this stage, our directive definition has been updated to the following:

```
...
scope : {
  'elements' : '=contentGrid',
  'userOptions' : '=options'
},
require : 'contentGrid',
controller : function ($scope, $element, $attrs) {
  var ctrl = this;

  var defaults = {
    columns : 4,//How many columns should we have
```

```
    columnWidth : 0,//Set this to force a specific column width,
instead of calculating based on columns property
    gutter : 0
  };

  ctrl.options = angular.extend({}, defaults, $scope.userOptions ||
{});
},
link : function ($scope, $element, $attrs, ctrl) {
  if ($scope.elements.length) {
    setTimeout(initOrUpdateMasonry);
  };

  var initialized = false;
  var initOrUpdateMasonry = function () {
    if (!initialized) {
      var opts = {
        columnWidth : ctrl.options.columnWidth || ($element.width() /
ctrl.options.columns),
        itemSelector : '.grid-element',
        gutter : ctrl.options.gutter
      };
      initialized = $element.masonry(opts);
    } else {
      //Already initialized, just update
      $element.masonry('reloadItems');
      $element.masonry('layout');
    }
  };

  $scope.$watch('elements', function (newValue, oldValue) {
    //Check to confirm that we actually have an array of elements to
work with
    if (newValue) {
      initOrUpdateMasonry();
    };
  });
}
...
```

To see the full code at this point, use `git checkout masonryConnected` to update your repository directory. Note that we've provided an `options` attribute property to allow users to pass in a map of options much like they normally would to a jQuery plugin, and we can extend it with our own defaults and then pass it along to the plugin. Whenever you're creating an integration between Angular and a plugin, I highly recommend you follow this pattern, as otherwise you'll find yourself adding several attributes and flags to account for control of each option, instead of a single map to handle all of them. We also setup our `initOrUpdateMasonry` method to properly apply our plugin options and also request that Masonry update its internal cache of items and then apply a new layout. If you prefer, you can split the `initOrUpdate` method into two separate calls, or even call the initialize portion immediately upon loading your directive, however when working with a plugin such as Masonry that doesn't perform any action until we actually have HTML content for it to work on, I prefer to delay initialization as long as possible. In my experience that leads to more performant applications, since the browser doesn't have to hold any additional objects or functions in memory until they're actually useful.

Testing Masonry

At this point we want to begin testing our plugin integration itself. Masonry doesn't provide any direct data-model changes that we can use to cleanly validate it via unit tests, so now seems like a good time to begin our E2E testing process. We want to validate our basic directive compilation as before, but also confirm that the grid elements are being modified by Masonry, which results in the three following tests:

```
describe('Content Grid', function () {
  beforeEach(function () {
    browser().navigateTo('/examples/');
  });

  it('should contain compiled content grid', function () {
    var grid = element('.content-grid');
    expect(grid.count()).toBe(1) ;
  });

  it('should contain two grid elements', function () {
    expect(element('.grid-element').count()).toBe(2);
  }) ;
```

```
    it('should have applied masonry', function () {
        expect(element('.grid-element:first').css('position')).
toBe('absolute')
    }) ;
});
```

The first thing you'll notice is that I'm using my examples directory as my test basis. While sometimes a specific test HTML file is more appropriate and/or cleaner, I find that using my examples directory as my E2E testing directory helps ensure that not only is my directive/application fully tested, but also that all the examples I provide to other developers are fully functional and correct as well. It also has the reverse effect of making sure my examples cover all the major functionality, since I want all of those pieces to be tested.

Next, take a look at the third test. This one will be different for every plugin you integrate. Some will add a class—those are some of the easiest to test. Some, such as Masonry, require that you test for a specific attribute or characteristic. While this isn't quite as clean and stable as testing for a specific class, unless you intend on absolutely positioning your elements manually, which begs the question of why you're even using Masonry in the first place, this kind of test will still suffice.

Events

When we first started this chapter, we said that we wanted to be able to hook into specific events. Masonry itself only provides two events, one when everything is laid out and one when an item is removed. Instead of Masonry events then, we'll create our own, starting with one for when it's first initialized, and another that fires anytime there's an update. Per usual, let's go ahead and write our unit tests first and then we'll update the directive code to satisfy them:

```
describe('Events', function () {
    var initEvent = 'masonry-initialized'
      , updateEvent = 'masonry-updated';

    it('should not fire ' + initEvent + ' event when initialized with no
elements', function () {
        var $parScope = $rootScope.$new();
        var initialized = false;
        $parScope.$on(initEvent, function () {
            initialized = true;
        });
```

```
      var $el = $compile(tpl)($parScope);
      $rootScope.$digest();
      expect(initialized).toBe(false);
    }) ;


    it('should fire ' + initEvent + ' event when initialized with
  elements', function () {
      var $parScope = $rootScope.$new();
      $parScope.elements = [ … ]
      var initialized = false;
      runs(function () {
        $parScope.$on(initEvent, function () {
          initialized = true;
        });
        var $el = $compile(tpl)($parScope);
        $rootScope.$digest();
      });
      waitsFor(function () {
        return initialized;
      }, 'Initialized should have been fired', 200);
      runs(function () {
        expect(initialized).toBe(true);
      })
    });


    /* … Repeat for update event ... */
  });
```

I've introduced a few new Jasmine testing methods here and if you're not accustomed to asynchronous testing within Jasmine, you likely haven't seen `runs` and `waitsFor` blocks before. Because the Angular `$emit` and `$broadcast` methods happen asynchronously, we need to run the code that should trigger the message within a run block, then tell Jasmine to wait until `initialized` returns `true` or 200 milliseconds pass, whichever comes first. If we time-out before `initialized` has been set to `true`, the second parameter gets passed back as a failure message.

For the sake of space, I'll let you implement the messaging system on your own, although of course if you need a guide you can checkout the `messagingEvents` git tag to see our final code.

Timing

I mentioned earlier that one of the reasons why I like using my examples directory as my basis for all E2E tests is that it helps ensure the quality of my code and my examples at the same time. As a prime example of this, when I added a logging element to my examples so I could demonstrate the use of our new initialized and updated events, I discovered that Masonry wasn't running quite as seamlessly as I'd originally imagined. The log was positioned right in the middle of the content grid, even though our elements extended far below that point. It turns out that even though Masonry was accurately positioning our elements, it was operating before all the element content had been compiled, and thus it miscalculated the proper height to apply to our grid. I noted in the first few chapters that any time you're applying a DOM manipulation plugin, it's often best to wrap it in a setTimeout method to ensure it operates after the compilation process it done. I had, however, forgotten to follow that advice when first setting everything up, and so while our content-grid element was ready for manipulation, the internal content-grid-element directives were still compiling and thus were not yet at their full height.

Wrapping the initOrUpdateMasonry method was simple enough; if you look at the code you just checked out you'll see that our watcher now includes the setTimeout wrapper. I also wanted to ensure I didn't somehow break that layout again later, however, so I added one more additional E2E test to finalize Version 1 of our new directive.

```
...
it('should have sized masonry correctly', function () {
  var maxElHeight = 0;
  element('.grid-element').query(function (elements, done) {
    elements.each(function (idx) {
      var el = elements.eq(0);
      var elHeight = el.outerHeight();
      if (elHeight > maxElHeight) {
        maxElHeight = elHeight;
      };
    });
    done();
  });
  expect(element('.content-grid').outerHeight())
    .not().toBeLessThan(maxElHeight)
})
```

The `element().query(fn)` method is provided by the Angular Scenario Runner and allows you to execute a function with the selected elements as your first parameter. Just be sure to call `done()`, the second parameter, at the end of your callback function, as this lets the Scenario Runner know that it can continue its tests. This test's setup still isn't perfect, since if we have several rows of content it might still pass. Most developers will tell you that it's impossible to perfectly test everything, especially when dealing with the browser directly, but at least this helps ensure that our internal compilation has progressed prior to Masonry resetting the layout.

Further steps

With that, we'll conclude our walkthrough of the development of a directive, however there are of course several other features and improvements left to add. If you want to experiment on your own, a few starting ideas might include adding the ability to transclude existing content elements into your grid or even allow certain elements to be *stamped*, which is Masonry's term for gluing one or more elements in place and then laying everything else out around them. Finally, if you want to experiment with controllers, try replacing our `elements` watcher statement with a controller function that each element directive calls when it initializes and ensure that the `initOrUpdateMasonry` method only fires when all the elements are ready. If you're really adventurous, you can even use Masonry's `appended` and `prepended` methods instead of `reloadItems` so that Masonry knows exactly how to update its layout more appropriately. And of course, if you want to join in on the live development of this or other Angular plugins, the development community is always open to new contributions.

Summary

Well, I hope you've enjoyed the ride through this book as much as I've enjoyed writing it, and hopefully I've managed to whet your appetite for even more AngularJS and data-driven modularity going forward. Angular is an extremely feature-full framework, and even as I was writing this book I discovered a multitude of new capabilities and development paradigms that furthered my coding processes. There are significant areas we haven't even touched. Services, in particular, deserve a mini-book of their own. I highly encourage you, whether it's with Angular, another framework, or a different language entirely, to continue experimenting and diving deeper into the world of problem solving through code. Thanks again for reading. You can find me online at `http://www.mrvdot.com`; please don't hesitate to contact me there with any questions or suggestions you might have.

Index

P

priority function 31
priority option 22

R

replace property 23
require property 26

S

Scenario Runner 72
scenarios, E2E testing 73, 74
Scope - {}
  & - method binding 44, 46
  @ - read-only Access 41-43
  = - two-way binding 43, 44
scope object 37
scope property
  false value 38, 39
  true value 40
setTimeout method 91

T

template property 23
templateUrl property 23
terminal option 23
Test Driven Development (TDD) 67
testing 65
test subject 71, 72
transclude 59
transcluded content
  manipulating 62, 63
transclude function 31
transclusion 27, 59, 60, 61
true value, scope property 40

U

unit testing 68, 69

W

web applications
  designing 5

Thank you for buying
AngularJS Directives

About Packt Publishing

Packt, pronounced 'packed', published its first book "*Mastering phpMyAdmin for Effective MySQL Management*" in April 2004 and subsequently continued to specialize in publishing highly focused books on specific technologies and solutions.

Our books and publications share the experiences of your fellow IT professionals in adapting and customizing today's systems, applications, and frameworks. Our solution based books give you the knowledge and power to customize the software and technologies you're using to get the job done. Packt books are more specific and less general than the IT books you have seen in the past. Our unique business model allows us to bring you more focused information, giving you more of what you need to know, and less of what you don't.

Packt is a modern, yet unique publishing company, which focuses on producing quality, cutting-edge books for communities of developers, administrators, and newbies alike. For more information, please visit our website: www.packtpub.com.

About Packt Open Source

In 2010, Packt launched two new brands, Packt Open Source and Packt Enterprise, in order to continue its focus on specialization. This book is part of the Packt Open Source brand, home to books published on software built around Open Source licences, and offering information to anybody from advanced developers to budding web designers. The Open Source brand also runs Packt's Open Source Royalty Scheme, by which Packt gives a royalty to each Open Source project about whose software a book is sold.

Writing for Packt

We welcome all inquiries from people who are interested in authoring. Book proposals should be sent to author@packtpub.com. If your book idea is still at an early stage and you would like to discuss it first before writing a formal book proposal, contact us; one of our commissioning editors will get in touch with you.

We're not just looking for published authors; if you have strong technical skills but no writing experience, our experienced editors can help you develop a writing career, or simply get some additional reward for your expertise.

Ext JS 4 Web Application Development Cookbook

ISBN: 978-1-849516-86-0   Paperback: 488 pages

Over 110 easy-to-follow recipes backed up with real-life examples, walking you through basic Ext JS features to advanced application design using Sencha's Ext JS

1. Learn how to build Rich Internet Applications with the latest version of the Ext JS framework in a cookbook style

2. From creating forms to theming your interface, you will learn the building blocks for developing the perfect web application

3. Easy to follow recipes step through practical and detailed examples which are all fully backed up with code, illustrations, and tips

Ext JS 4 First Look

ISBN: 978-1-849516-66-2   Paperback: 340 pages

A practical guide including examples of the new features in Ext JS 4 and tips to migrate from Ext JS 3

1. Migrate your Ext JS 3 applications easily to Ext JS 4 based on the examples presented in this guide

2. Full of diagrams, illustrations, and step-by-step instructions to develop real word applications

4. Driven by examples and explanations of how things work

Please check **www.PacktPub.com** for information on our titles

CPSIA information can be obtained at www.ICGtesting.com
Printed in the USA
LVOW05s1933030614

388429LV00013B/665/P